Lindsay Rudland is 72; a retired nurse following 46 years in clinical practice – 30 of them in mental health care. Born when rationing was still in place, she has lived through the austere 50s when listening to the radio was a highlight. Through the 60s, being part of the counter culture and surviving blooded but unbowed through the following decades. A single parent. She has maintained her enthusiasm for this precious life through friendships, self-help and yoga, despite promiscuity, bereavements financial hardship, failed relationships and frequent irresponsibility.

*This book is dedicated to Sadhguru
and all seekers after the truth.*

Lindsay Rudland

ENDEAVOUR TO RISE – MISDEMEANOURS, MUSINGS, MEDITATIONS, MISTAKES AND MASTERY

AUSTIN MACAULEY PUBLISHERS™

LONDON • CAMBRIDGE • NEW YORK • SHARJAH

A CIP catalogue record for this title is available from the British Library.

ISBN 9781398405479 (Paperback)
ISBN 9781528900959 (Hardback)
ISBN 9781398405011 (ePub e-book)

www.austinmacauley.com

First Published 2022
Austin Macauley Publishers Ltd®
1 Canada Square
Canary Wharf
London
E14 5AA

I would like to acknowledge my dear sister, Deborah, for her un-ending love and support. My dear friend, Sarah, for typing the manuscript and inspiring the subtitle. Hotel staff at the beautiful Avisford Park Hotel where I wrote a lot of the book, the front cover is me in the grounds.

Table of Contents

Is your life full on?
Or are you on standby?

If you want to be Fully Alive – don't buy this book –
go online, find Sadhguru and buy his book:

Inner Engineering
A Yogi's Guide to Joy
Do the online course:
Inner Engineering

If you want to know about the efforts this author has made
to get happy – read on.

I will give you a true account of my experiences as none
of my efforts worked for me, well, not in the long term.

Then I will tell you what did work for me.

We are all pursuing more; more pleasure, more money,
more power, more knowledge and more comfort.
Sadhguru

If you have tried everything or preferably before you try
everything.
Sadhguru

Sadhguru reminds us that we are the most privileged generation ever. We have more technology, more comfort than was ever imagined, however are we the most joyful, healthy, peaceful, productive and inclusive generation ever?

It is not working; wars, starvation, mass migration, suffering, exploitation, stress, fear and global degradation.

Where are we going wrong

If life is not happening the way you think it should happen – turn within.

You shouldn't be committed to the way someone else wants you to be.

You must be committed to the way you want to be.

Sadhguru

If you ever write a book about your life would you tell the truth, the whole truth or would you hesitate?

I certainly did.

If you have a family, would you seek to protect them from the unvarnished truth or would you stay true to your own experience?

It is said what is withheld increases and what is shared releases.

Efforts to be opaque may be an attempt to protect one's public persona and avoid censure, excoriation, libel, trolling and all the other ills which social media has spawned.

An act of sharing carries with it concern for others, e.g. those who were party to my actions. They are all blameless but they may not wish to be reminded of their part in the drama; or those close to me may be deeply embarrassed by some of my revelations.

I decided to tell it like it is (Why bowdlerise your own life?)!

Thomas Bowdler (1754–1825) was an English physician known for publishing *The Family Shakespeare,* a censored version of Shakespeare plays that would be more suitable to be read by ladies and children.

There are some omissions, mostly to avoid tedium.

My intention is to share my own experiences in order that those who wish to read my account may ponder the ramifications and, if they so choose, use my suggestions to gain insight, enliven and enhance their own lives.

We are all on a one-way ticket. We are in Heaven right here and we are making a Hell of it.

When you realise that you share 50% of your genetic material with a banana, why take life too seriously?

Chapter 1: My Origins

(In Brief)

Things I learned at my mother's knee and other low joints.

Life is a mystery and a miracle.

'A miracle is an event so unlikely as to be almost impossible.
By that definition I've just proved that you are a miracle.'
– Dr Ali Binazir

In a recent talk at Ted X, Mel Robbins, a self-help author, mentioned that scientists estimate that the probability of you being born is about 1 in 400 trillion. Dr Binazir reflected on this and then blogged about it.

Factored in is the chance of your parents meeting – then the chance of them speaking, then the chance of them getting pregnant.

Each sperm and each egg is genetically unique because of the process of meiosis. A fertile woman had approximately 100,00 viable eggs on average. A man will produce about 525 billion sperm cells over a lifetime and shed at least one billion of them a month in the course of his reproductive lifetime.

A healthy adult male can release between 40 million and 1.2 billion sperm cells in a single ejaculation.

So, the probability of that one sperm cell with half your name on it, meeting that one egg with the other half of your name on it is one in 400 quadrillion.

Also consider that the existence of you here now on planet earth presupposes another supremely unlikely and undeniable chain of events. That is, that all your ancestors lived to a reproductive age – going all the way back to not just the first Homo Sapiens, first Homo Erectus and Homohabilis, but all the way back to the first single-celled organism. You are a representative of an unbroken lineage of life going back four billion years. (Get into it: are you a miracle? Dr Ali Binazir, HuffPost contributor.

Did I feel like a miracle? No!

I was reared by two fearful and disappointed people; fearful because they knew what it meant to be swept up in circumstances beyond their control. We have all experienced that as children, where other people made the rules before you got there and you had to fit in with them.

However, in recent times we have not been caught up in circumstances as cataclysmic as two World Wars. They were disappointed because life didn't turn out the way they wanted.

They were also fiercely loyal, hard-working and loving.

Ron and Peggy

The butcher's boy and the bowls club secretary's daughter. My mum and dad were born in 1912 and 1913 respectively. His dad was a stockman who died when Dad was seven. He left his widow to bring up three children; dad his

15

sister Daphne and his brother George, who appeared to have learning difficulties, but maybe was just failed by the education system.

Mum was part of a large family, one of eight children, seven of whom survived into their 60s or 70s. Mum's dad worked for the Prudential Insurance Company and he owned properties that had been built by his father.

Mum's dad was secretary of the local bowling club, he was a school governor, teetotal and loved touring in his bull-nosed Morris Oxford. The car got its name from its distinctive round-topped radiator at first called the bullet nose.

He was well-read and a champion of the free press. He wrote a small autobiography. He called it 'the autobiography of a very ordinary man', but I bet he didn't think he was very ordinary.

Grandad didn't mention my mother once by name in his autobiography – he just wrote, 'When we lived in Hove, we had three more children, two girls and a boy.'

I don't know how distant he was as a father, but I think that may give us a clue. Interestingly, his earliest memory was of living with his aunty, his mother's sister (his mother died when Grandad was three). His dad eventually married his aunty but they had to get married in Switzerland where the marriage of the deceased wife's sister was legal.

His dad had a shop on Chapel Green, Crowborough – the house he was born in. Grandad's father retired in 1893 and had two properties built and bought some cottages – then he had Studleigh built – a lovely house, still there in Queens Road, which became the main family home. He was the only grandparent that saw me, I think he held me after I was born in 1947, but he died later that year. All my other grandparents were deceased years before. Mum was born with a caul a piece of the amniotic sac still attached to the head. Easily removed it is said to prevent drowning and some sailors wore a dried caul for that purpose; I don't know how that superstition evolved.

School picture 9 years old

Mum was educated at Varndean High School for Girls – a prestigious school, having been established in 1884, and still here today. She matriculated (sounds painful) and went into secretarial college where her typing and Pitman's shorthand were exemplary.

My dad was schooled locally in Crowborough and left at 14, having garnered little in academic terms. He was apprenticed to the local butcher and stayed in that trade for the rest of his life. There was very little money. His widowed mother, Ada, took in washing and his sister did a lot of parenting.

Dad used to deliver meat to Mum's house, he always described himself as 'the little boy that Santa Claus forgot', and always carried a feeling of lack or deprivation. His one piece of advice to me was, 'Get a good job with a pension.'

Dad became a skilled butcher and worked long hours in cold conditions for other people. He always voted Tory for the deep ideological reason that he thought they would take six pence off income tax. He could have had a shop of his own, he was offered sponsorship. I'm sure he was investable, skilled and hard-working, but he lacked self-belief and, consequently, any aspiration to rise up.

His faith, if he had any in divine intervention, was dashed when, as a little boy at Sunday School he and the other children were asked to pray for something and were then invited to share what they had prayed for. Dad had prayed for a goat and when he shared that with the class the Sunday School teacher slapped him. Presumably this was because he should have prayed for something else, such as forgiveness or humility, or world peace. I'm not sure he ever understood what he had done wrong and, when I think about this incident, I always cry for my dad.

He always said he went to the church where the prayer books had handles – i.e. the pub. I'm sure he got more solace there than in a church, as do a lot of people.

He did say the only religious group that ever meant anything to him was the Salvation Army as they helped his mum and they were very present in the war years. We had an officer from the Salvation Army to conduct his funeral.

I love the idea of the Salvation Army, which was started by William and Catherine Booth in 1865. The came out of the church and took God's word to the people. They lived out their doctrine of practical Christianity – soup, soap and salvation. They set up shelters for the homeless, traced families, ran soup kitchens, set up homes for women fleeing abuse and prostitution. They oversaw the world's first free labour exchange and campaigned to improve working conditions.

It was named the Salvation Army in 1878, having previously been called the Christian Mission.

Sadly, the same problems are still with us and the Army is active all over the world, serving in over 130 countries, offering hope and love to all those in need, without discrimination. That to me is the nearest you'd get, if you believed in a God, to actually living your faith. If I was religious, I would join them as opposed to any other religious set up and I think I'd look good in a bonnet.

When I was two we were very fortunate to get a council house. A really lovely red brick, three bedroomed semi-detached house, with a large garden front and back. When I was growing up, Dad who was a son of the soil (they were mostly farming folk in East Sussex) maintained the gardens, on top of his long working days. We had beautifully sculpted hedges, not topiary as such, but undulating privet hedges, lawns, lovely flower beds – he loved pansies with their little faces.

There was also a big vegetable garden separated from the lawn by a rockery, so we had a lot of fresh produce, carrots, peas, onions, runner beans, potatoes and strawberries. I remember eating the new peas out of the pod – there is nothing like freshly picked vegetables.

I never realised how much work it takes to maintain a garden and it is not until a gardener dies that you can fully appreciate the full impact of what they did.

I am so proud of my father and all that he did for us. When we were quite young, he had a benign brain tumour and was not expected to live, he was just wasting away in hospital until our GP suggested Dad may have a neurological problem and he was transferred up to Queens Square in London, where he was operated on by an eminent neurosurgeon, Dr Wylie McKissock (he later became Sir Wylie McKissock).

The operation was a success, but it left my father with a problem with his balance which meant he had to give up his golf and cricket which he loved. Crowborough has a really well-known golf links, I used to walk around there with him.

I am so grateful to Sir Wylie for helping my dad but as a mental health nurse I loathe him as he carried out over 3,000 frontal lobotomies, he was apparently a very enthusiastic lobotomiser. I know they were different times, but it is a cautionary tale. It is amazing the power we invest in our doctors and the power they take unto themselves.

In my next book entitled *Who Cares?* I will be sharing my experiences in 46 years of nursing, most of it in mental health and talking about the uses and abuses of psychiatry.

Dad died when he was 66. We lived in Worthing and he had gone to his birthplace Crowborough to visit his brother and sister-in-law. He washed and dressed on that particular morning and sat down to have a cup of tea and just passed away peacefully in the chair. It was as if he had gone home to die, he never even drew his pension.

I think his lifetime consumption of meat may well have contributed to his demise leading to arteriosclerosis, he had had a small stroke previously. It is ironic that meat and the meat trade sustained him and our family in life but was implicated in his early death.

Suffice to say I am a vegetarian.

My mother was a lioness (Leo) in the house and a mouse outside of it. Brought up in a certain tradition, she was what we used to call a 'snob' i.e. a person who believes that their tastes in a particular area are superior to those of other people.

Unfortunately, when I was old enough to experience fully the interactions between my parents, I could sense that, to my mother, Daddy was inferior. This had a profound effect on me as the eldest child and I am still trying to overcome its taint as it did damage my relationships with the opposite sex.

Mummy was well-read and we had a lot of books in the house in a lovely glass-fronted bookcase. She loved opera and poetry. I still have a copy of her favourite anthology, Palgrave's *Golden Treasury*, a wonderful collection. One of my mother's favourite poems in that collection is 'Bridge of Sighs', it is about a woman who commits suicide by drowning – an intriguing choice and a beautiful poem, 'Take her up tenderly' is a phrase she particularly loved.

Whilst Mummy loved books, I never saw my dad read one; he liked *Tit Bits* and *News of the World*.

Mum was an avid crossword solver, the cryptic ones. I have never mastered that skill. She hated to be beaten and would trawl through our set of encyclopaedias looking for answers. We loved puns or a play on words and we would often carry on a theme for ages, e.g. I can't see the wood for the trees, leaf it out, I'm branching out, I'm making a trunk call, I'm going out on a limb, oh, I twig on to what you are doing, and so on and on!

Mummy absolutely loved the natural world, especially animals and birds. We three kids had a love of nature and all creatures instilled in us. Once, my mother reared a baby starling; she used a little eyedropper to feed it and, as it grew, she would stand on the furniture, holding it up, urging it to fly, then it would sit on top of the kitchen cupboard for a while until she finally released it back into the wild. She called it 'Stanley' and it used to come back for some years and sit on the kitchen windowsill. Once, she saved a baby sparrow which had been found in a drain with some twine around its feet (people used to bring the injured birds to Mum), and it did survive. Another time, she removed a large tick from our dog. It was rounded in shape and was a bulbous thing in a greyish colour, it looked like a small, rounded pebble. Mum kept it in a matchbox. She kept looking at it and often invited us to look as well, she was so fascinated by it. I suppose it was engorged with the dog's blood as it stayed alive for a week or two. This was very irresponsible as they are nasty things and can cause Lyme disease. My dad used to call her an evil old witch and said her cats were her familiars. She had four at one time and he was fearful that the council might come and throw us out of the house.

She would never kill anything, if a wasp or a bee got inside the house, she would open the window and invite them to leave. Spiders were never to be killed, she used to say, 'If you want to live and thrive, let the spider run alive.' She also used to quote from the Bible, 'Go to the ant, thou sluggard, consider her ways and be wise.' I'm not sure which book it is in. I still say these things to my grandchildren, when you consider how ants live it is such a brilliant comment on community cohesion and sustainability.

Once, my sister Deborah went round to see Mum and she picked some peonies from the garden to take back to her place. When she got home, she saw an ant crawl out of one of the peonies; she put it in a matchbox and drove all the way back to Mum's and put it back on the peony plant.

"It must have its family there," said Sis.

I love that story so much and I love my sister deeply.

Mum was a mistress of one-liners and she could also wither you with one look or dismiss you with a well-chosen epithet. When I got engaged, she barely glanced at the ring, she felt I could do better, I suppose, and she said of my fiancé, 'He's so passive, he's inert.' Of another boyfriend she said, 'He is rather effete.' Mind you, she wasn't usually far wrong.

Some of her remarks stay in family history – I guess all families have a joke or saying that is passed down the generations. Some of ours were: 'If you happen to find yourself upstairs could you bring me my blue cardigan.'

One old uncle used to always take the left-over dessert, he would just put it on his plate saying, "Nobody wants any more if this, do they?" He just gave a glance to everyone, not intending to share. We had an electric meter and the shilling would often run out and plunge us into darkness, then we used to say, 'Where was Moses when the light went out?' and then in unison, 'In the dark!'. We bought Mum a toaster once, as she always used the grill pan in the oven. We made her some toast thinking she would like our gift – her response: 'I want toast, not warmed bread!'

23

Once, my brother was eating his lunch on the shed roof, we used to climb up there when Mum and Dad were at work and we were on school holidays. We had a nosy neighbour two doors away, she was like Hyacinth Bucket, very proper and inordinately house-proud. Her two kids were never allowed to play out in the street with the rest of us rabble – there were a good few kids in the neighbourhood as the council houses were given to families, obviously I think they suffered a bit under a strict regime. When her husband came home from work, he had to whistle a tune as he came up the garden path so she knows it was him – go figure!

Anyway, she saw my brother on the shed roof and said, "You shouldn't be up there. I'll tell your mother when she gets home from work."

Peter told her, " mind your own bloody business."

When Mum got home, he told her the neighbour may visit and what had passed between them. Mum prepared a suitable response in anticipation of the neighbour's visit. She waited a couple of days but the neighbour never came round.

Mum never got a chance to give her response, she was going to say, "I agree with his sentiments, but I deplore his lack of manners."

A great line; I bet she would not have said it anyway, she was too much of a wimp in public, but the line has gone into family history.

When I was about ten my mother had pneumonia (I remember having that in a spelling lesson at junior school, when I was about seven, and sounding the 'p'.) I can recall them having a stand-up row in their bedroom because she would not go into the hospital and Dad was insisting that she should go.

Mum was treated with Penicillin, which she maintained saved her life. It only became more widely used to treat infection from the mid-40s onwards, although it was discovered in 1928 it was not until 1944 that commercial production began in earnest. This was in 1957 so it was fairly early days.

I had to take a couple of weeks off school to 'look after her' and do a bit of housekeeping.

The neighbours were great, bringing us some prepared food and checking on us. The aforesaid nosy neighbour made us some lovely scones with raisins. Accompanying the scones was little itemised bill, e.g. 8oz flour 2/-, 2oz raisins 30d, 3oz butter one shilling, etc. Dad paid it when he got home from work. It made us laugh, nobody else asked for money they just gave us stuff.

Mum and Dad met at the tennis club, he said the first thing he noticed about her were her 'bats', i.e. legs, getting out of the car. I think they had to share a court as it was busy. I guess theirs was initially a passionate affair, but it eventually went sour. She wanted Ronald Colman and he thought a woman was there to love and nurture him (as had his mum and his sister). I have some of their correspondence from the early years and they are overflowing with love and desire.

They were married for 12 years before I, their first child, came along; the war years having intervened. Dad served in Africa and Italy. I think he had what they call a 'Good War'. He was driving officers around in a jeep. I don't think he saw much combat and I think he had a fling in Italy with a woman called Gina.

Dad originally applied for the air force but was not accepted. However, when he discovered that the average life expectancy for a rear gunner was 15 minutes, he was glad he was rejected.

My mum and dad were victims of a certain social structure, a particular education system and certain religious ideologies. It's hard to think for yourself under the weight of all that clutter. Plus, two World Wars, which were testimony to human beings' blinding ignorance and inability to learn from history, and you end up with two people who are fearfully disappointed, believing that there is more to life, but not knowing how to get it.

Dad used to say, "When my ship comes in."

He was meaning things will change for the better, but he was waiting for it to happen; he certainly wasn't creating change. Eventually he used to say that his ship had got lost at sea.

My mother must have had a strict moral code programmed into her as she suffered awful guilt and shame. When I arrived, after their 12 years of marriage, it coincided with the death of my grandfather, so Mum inherited some money. Mum's sister, my aunty Connie who was a teacher, advised her to buy a house. They were about £1,000 in 1947, but Mum just spent it all.

My brother arrived in 1949 and then my sister in 1951. Mum said she would have had more because they never used contraception, but it didn't happen. I think the desire had gone away, as the money ran out and the family grew, the passion cooled and the novelty wore off.

When I was 34 my mother told me that she felt guilty about my sister's birth as she had 'not been conceived in love'. Imagine suffering such guilt for decades, and where did she get such an idea? How many of us have been 'conceived in love'? It's mostly lust or accident!

Apparently, Dad had come home from the pub one evening, he never got really inebriated, anyway they must have had sex, but Mum didn't consider herself to be in the right emotional state in which a child should be conceived. Mother's guilt so blighted her relationship with my sister that Deb always felt that she was adopted.

When I was born there was a telegram sent to my dad in Worthing, as Mum was in Crowborough visiting her father. It was from my aunty Janet, Mum's sister, announcing my arrival (I still have it). There were loads of photographs and a posh christening in the local church with lovely photographs. I have a baby book with entries recording my birth weight, etc. the names of the doctor and midwives who were in attendance. It also has a record of my first steps, first words and a lock of my hair.

By the time my sister arrived the money had run out and there were two toddlers to deal with and the love between my mum and dad had faded. There were no photos of her as a baby and only a piece of paper with some of her birth details written in pencil. No wonder Deb felt she had arrived by adoption!

Mum told me not to tell Deborah, but of course, I did. The result was so dramatic for my sister, the veil had been lifted and the truth was revealed, the truth can set you free.

My sister was joyful at this revelation, she was by then a mother herself and it transformed her relationship with Mum. Sadly, she never did have the conversation with Mum, so she carried it to the grave.

Fete 6 years old, in school fete fancy dress as the queen of hearts

My mother also felt she was being punished because she had spent the money that we kids had raised by staging a garden fete for charity. We often did that in school holidays; we would sell lemonade, make games for people to play like quoits or 'Aunt Sally' – once we staged a play in my mate Ros's Garden. We draped blankets over the washing-line as curtains and then pulled them aside to start the performance. I can't remember the play but I remember one of my lines: 'In heraldry blue is referred to as azure.' Funny, what you retain, eh?

We raised £9 for St Dunstan's but it never got sent as Mum spent it, we were so cash strapped. Bless her, she felt so guilty and that she was being punished.

I sent them a big donation when I could, to make up for it. (Incidentally, one of the workshops I offer is about letting go of blame and shame, and I combine it with laughing yoga.) I feel letting go should be a joy and not a traumatic exercise. Recognise it. Own it and let go. The workshop is entitled *Forget Blame and Shame, get in the Game* [That is, the game of life]. There are T-shirts as well! See website for details.

All in all, those early years were great – our garden backed onto the railway line and of course it was steam trains in those days so we could wave at the drivers, like 'The Railway Children', and they always waved back.

Our milk was delivered in glass bottles by a milkman with a horse-drawn float and left on the doorstep. If we were fortunate, the horse would leave some manure for the garden. We had to compete for it, though, with other kids!

A coalman would come, carrying a sack of coal on his shoulders and hurl the coal into the coal-cellar. I think the sacks of coal weighed about a hundredweight, i.e. 50.8 kg.

The dustmen had to pick up a metal dustbin and chuck the contents in the dustcart. I don't think we generated so much waste in those days.

Folk would call at the door selling cockles and mussels and a lorry would come round regularly delivering Hooper Struve pop like Cream Soda, Dandelion and Burdock and lemonade – they had really nice bottles with those flip tops.

It is a shame the recycling of milk bottles has pretty much gone but now you can order virtually anything online and have it delivered to your door.

Being a council house, every two years or so some painters would come to decorate the doors and window-frames. We had Fred and Sam, they were lovely guys and we used to climb up their ladder when we could get away with it. Look at the travesty of social housing that exists today and look at where it has led us. For example, property prices have rocketed as the housing stock is so low, foreign investors can buy so the prices become even more inflated. Buy to let has produced some greedy landlords, there is often sub-standard accommodation and children may be condemned to years in bed and breakfast with nowhere to call home where they can live and play securely.

Homelessness, rough sleepers, debt – shame, shame, shame.

I must admit to hypocrisy here – though against my principles I did buy our council house with Mum as I was pregnant and about to become a single parent with twins. I think the local council were supposed to use the proceeds to build more affordable properties but this didn't seem to happen.

The point of this book is to share the things I have done to get pleasure or be happy purely because they didn't work for me, not in the long run, anyway – well, maybe some of them did. I was very fortunate not to be caught stealing as it may have caused, a different outcome for my life.

I have come to realise that others who try these activities may find themselves stuck with them.

As my mum used to say: "Don't make that face, the wind may change and you'll be stuck with it."

Chapter 2: Masturbation

The first thing I consciously remember doing in order to get pleasure or relief or comfort was masturbation.

I think I was about six years old (apparently this is a common age for this behaviour). Meg Zweiback – bless her – a nurse practitioner from Oakland, California, says masturbation in young children isn't sexual as it is for adults because young children don't know what sex is. They masturbate because it feels good.

I masturbated to orgasm excessively with panting, red face and a big sigh at the end. I had multiple orgasms and even did it in junior school once in a music lesson.

Apparently, excessive masturbation may be a sign of anxiety, being emotionally overwhelmed or not getting enough attention at home; this is according to the American Academy of Paediatrics. This must signal my emotional state, but I have no clear recollection of what was going on in my mind other than guilt and shame inculcated in me by my mother.

On reflection I do see that tensions were arising in Mum and Dad's life and relationship. There was little money and I now had my two younger siblings. Mum said I helped her when they were babies, so I guess I did have a lot to deal with.

Apparently, masturbation is like nose picking, which I also did a lot of. It can stem from boredom, because our hands are free and because we can. Parents reactions to masturbation may pose the greatest danger for children. If one is made to feel guilty for exploring your body, or made to feel it is dirty or naughty, we may associate sexual or pleasurable feelings with guilt and shame. If a parent is really bothered by it, Zweiback says, it probably suggests more about what the parent learned growing up than it does about the child.

My mother kept telling me off about it, she called it my 'filthy habit'; she said, 'If you keep doing that, you'll never have a baby.'

Exploring your physicality and finding it pleasurable is not wrong or unclean or uncommon. However, when it gets stuck in your mind and equates to other people it can become a perversion.

There is a growing problem with young boys becoming addicted to porn, when they start seeking more extreme forms of sexual activity on the internet and it spills over into their relationships.

An alarming percentage of internet traffic is concerned with pornography. It is a tragic and dangerous distortion of male/female relationships, or – I wonder what La Gioconda's tits are like? Or you can fiddle with yourself while the planet burns!

The curiosity is not unusual or abnormal. When we were kids, we went through Dad's tallboy, he had some old pictures of naked woman engaged in fairly benign sexual acts – he must have carried them throughout the war years.

We looked at nudes in library books, then later we read the sex bits in *Lady Chatterley's Lover*. Now, the availability of pornography, much of it extreme and live, is causing young men to get stuck with it and blighting their relationships with women as it can become addictive.

Incidentally, at the moment of orgasm pain is obliterated. I used to use it as a palliative measure when I had toothache, which I suffered frequently due to poor dental hygiene. Sadly, the relief is very short-lived but it does work.

It also gives some relief from migraine, which I suffered from in my young years. Once when I was at Junior School, I had migraine (Migraine are very severe headaches with acute stabbing pain, often in the temple, also nausea and vomiting and photophobia). I was sent to the school sick room to lie down. I must have fallen asleep as I woke up around 4 p.m. and everybody had gone home, except the cleaners. The teacher had forgotten about me. I just got up and walked home.

In her book *Heal Your Body* Louise L Hay, a motivational author who popularised the mind/body theories that suggested symptoms or illness were the body's expression of unresolved unconscious processes. E.g. lower back pain is a fear of money and lack of financial support. Louise then gives an affirmation to assist one in recognising and resolving the problem. In this case it is 'I trust the process of life. All I need is always taken care of – I am safe'.

Her book came out in 1984 and I still refer to it regularly. I do recommend it if you wish to take responsibility for your own health. Louise says that migraine headaches, 'suggest dislike of being driven. Resisting the flow of life. Sexual fears (can usually be relieved by masturbation)'. The affirmation is, 'I relax into the flow of life and let life provide all that I need easily and comfortably. Life is for me.'

Masturbation still provokes criticism, disgust and insults and as it is pretty much a natural part of human development we should be more relaxed about it.

Chapter 3: Lying

'Oh, what a tangled web we weave when first we practice to deceive.'

Quote from the 1808 romantic poem Marmion by Sir Walter Scott.

It is thought that if you speak to someone for more than ten minutes, odds are that one of you was lying; and according to mashable.com if that person was your mother the odds of lying increase dramatically.

There is considerable neurological activity when one lies, the frontal lobe, the limbic system and the temporal lobe are all activated. We are aware of GSR i.e. Galvanic Skin Response technology or lie detection. We know a lie detector can be beaten but that just means the person is a really accomplished liar!

Commonly we lie to avoid punishment and this is regardless of age. I am sure you have been found out in a lie, just like the rest of us.

Just think of all the prominent people – politicians, clerics, doctors, lawyers, police officers and celebrities who have been found to be lying, often with the most devastating effects on innocent people.

I lied readily through decades of my life and still do at times. I like to think of them as 'white lies'. I lied so I could enhance my standing with people, presumably because I felt inadequate. I told people ('people'? – they were my friends!) that my dad was a vicar. I can't think why. When I got married my friends thought my dad would officiate – get out of that one!

I played truant from high school as I hated it. I was supposed to be doing 'A' Levels but I was never there. I was probably at home masturbating! I wanted to leave school before said 'A' Levels, so I typed a letter to that effect, traced my father's signature and put it at the foot of the letter. My parents never seemed to realise that I didn't take my 'A' Levels and didn't seem to enquire about the results. I think they were so consumed with their own problems they just didn't know what was going on with us kids.

I lied to my tutors in nursing school, I lied to my husband, I lied to my darling sister and, I guess, all the time I was lying to myself about who I was. I was great at false flattery and not being authentic with people. My sister is absolutely brilliant at speaking truth to power and has always been true to herself. It pained me so much when she was honest with me but 'wow' did it help me recognise my own failings. I so love that in her as well as so many other aspects of her character.

If you get stuck in this one it can lead to fraud, perjury, duplicity and criminality. You could be a conman/woman, a bigamist, a forger but you would be a million miles from your true self. Just consider the prominent people who have lied in public in recent times; e.g. Bernie Madoff, financier who duped investors out of billions of dollars before his Ponzi scheme collapsed. Richard Nixon and Watergate, Roman

Catholic clergy and child abusers, Cecil Parkinson and his affair with Sarah Keays and Jonathan Aitken MP jailed for perjury in 1997. We all lie but not all lies are the same; people lie and tell the truth to achieve a goal.

"We lie if honesty won't work," says researcher Tim Levine.

I think I started to consciously try to stop lying after I did the EST training, but more of that later.

Chapter 4: Stealing

The fundamental truth about stealing, whether in children or adults, is that your mind-set tells you that having something outside yourself will enhance your life, give you pleasure, help you feel better about yourself, raise your status amongst others, give yourself a sense of power or, more realistically, deprive someone else of their possession in order to inflict pain or loss or to fool them into feeling guilty for losing the item.

My earliest memory of stealing was when I was about seven or eight, I can't recall the exact age. I stole sixpence (that is six old pence) from my mum's purse, went to the shops and bought a Mars Bar. I was walking back home when Mum came pedalling up on her old bicycle to meet me.

I can still recall my visceral reaction to her question, "Did you take money from my purse?"

Now my mother watched every penny and accounted for it, writing everything down. We were very cash poor and every penny counted. As I write I think about my purse now, it is very heavy with loose chance (it got worse when we lost the ten-shilling note and then the pound note) I wouldn't know if 5p was missing. Mind you I am very irresponsible when it comes to money.

I said, "You can have the Mars Bar." (They cost 5d in those days, pre-decimalisation.)

Mum responded, in her most haughty tone, "I don't want the Mars Bar. I want the sixpence."

I think I ate the Mars Bar but somehow it didn't taste very good.

I did a paper round from the age of 13½ and worked in the shop after school. I stole comics, sweets and money from the till. I stole a purse from somebody's bag at a party and once stole a coat from a night club. I stole a copy of *The Rubaiyat of Omar Khayyam* from a friend – a friend!

There are probably other things, but I don't recall them.

Money is the main commodity that causes people to steal. It has always been equated with power, not least in present time when you can buy land, buy people, buy political influence and even buy an American Presidency.

Sometimes we seem to have a grudging admiration for those who carry out daring or audacious robberies, especially if it is deemed to be a blow against the establishment.

For example: The Great Train Robbery when, on 8th August 1963, £2.6 million (£5.3 value today) was stolen from a Royal Mail train. The perpetrators became celebrities and were only censured because of the attack on the train driver Jack Mills and the trackside assault on David Whitby who was a second man, i.e. an assistant to the driver. Look how we followed the exploits of Ronnie Biggs.

The establishment struck back by giving seven of the robbers 30 years in prison, you barely get half of that for murder these days.

Then there was the Brink's-Mat robbery. On 26th November 1983, a gang of masked robbers carried out Britain's largest ever robbery, at a warehouse belonging to the security company Brink's-Mat, at Heathrow Airport. It was an inside job and actually the perpetrators didn't realise there was gold bullion worth £26 million in the facility. Michael McAvoy and Anthony Black (the inside man) were caught and jailed for 25 years. About £10 million of the proceeds have never been recovered.

There has subsequently been various court cases and murders linked to the robbery. John Palmer, nicknamed 'Goldfinger', was implicated when he was found melting down gold in his garden. At trial he was acquitted when he claimed he was not aware that the gold was stolen. Palmer used to say, 'He who has the gold makes the rules.' He was shot dead by a hit man in 2015.

Some of the proceeds are said to have been used to develop the illegal supply of ecstasy, a new drug of the time, which was very profitable.

Acting out of clear intent is a very laudable quality and we are often urged to be goal directed. However, when it involves criminal acts, it is less than desirable. There is no pissing about with this type of stealing – you want something so you go for it, but you have no idea what you will unleash as a result.

My brother stole money from the old lodger that Mum took in to help our finances. He was a retired bank manager and a widower. I remember the crisp ten shilling notes my brother stole. I had five of them and bought a pair of shoes. Unfortunately, I had to hide them under the hedge in a plastic bag so Mum and Dad didn't see them. Nothing was ever said about the theft, but the lodger moved out.

I had a boyfriend who was a compulsive thief. He and his friend used to do a weekly shop in a little local corner shop. They called it a five-star dozy shop because it was so easy to rob. Buy a few things and steal a lot more.

Once they drove up to a hardware shop that was displaying a set of garden furniture on the forecourt. They folded it all up, put it in their car and drove off.

Another time we all went to London to see a weight-lifting competition, my sister was with his mate. On the way home we stopped at a pub and my boyfriend stole a radio from someone's car in the car park. Unknown to him I went and put it back. Later, as we were about to leave, he realised it was gone and went and re-stole it!

The boys had both been in Borstal and they ultimately both served time in prison. I wonder what they are doing now as this was the late 60's I am so relieved I didn't get stuck in this one. Many folks do, sadly, there is a very high rate of recidivism in the prison population.

I feel there is no pleasure in having something you have not obtained legitimately and I know the pain of having things stolen from me. I am too frightened to steal anything now.

The only times I felt I was robbed was I suppose when I robbed myself! When I think of my parlous history with credit cards and all the interest I have paid over the years, as a single parent I did resort to using credit cards to give my daughters what they wanted rather than being sensible.

I also think of being stuck with a 5% fixed rate mortgage, for five years, when the bank rate was peanuts! Mind you we must remember, the goal of the banking industry is to make everyone slaves to DEBT! Neither of my daughters have ever had a credit card, bizarrely I don't think that helps their credit rating .

Chapter 5: Eating

I was very fortunate to have good food as a child. My mum was a great cook and we had produced from Dad's garden, and joints of meat that were given as part of his wages as a butcher. I don't remember rejecting anything or being made to 'clear my plate' which some children were forced to do.

I do remember wanting more milk, as we only used to get a pint a day and I loved it, especially when it was really cold. Mind you, school milk was another matter. It came in $1/3$-pint bottles and had slivers of ice in it in the winter. In the summer it was often horrible and tepid but you could get to be milk monitor.

In those days we didn't have a fridge, just a walk-in larder with a marble shelf for the cold stuff. It seemed to work pretty well and, in those days, we ate fresh food and did not need to store it.

Mum used to make suet pudding that was steamed in a cloth. It was stodgy, cheap and filling and lovely with golden syrup. She sometimes made toffee, which was chemically exciting. You had to heat the sugar to just the right temperature and employed a sugar thermometer for that purpose.

Dad insisted on a roast dinner every Sunday. Mum prepared it while he went to the working men's club for a few beers. He only drank ½ pints – I don't know why. We had apple pie and cream every Sunday for dessert. I got fed up with beating the cream, just using a fork, to thicken it up – we didn't have an electric whisk then.

School dinners were another matter. I absolutely loved them and, when I was in junior school, I used to serve the teachers their dinner in the staff room. They used to watch me leave the room with the dirty plates on a tray, hooking my foot around the door to close it, as I didn't have a free hand. They thought I had good balance and coordination.

The food was cooked on the premises in a proper kitchen in those days. Now it is all pre-cooked chilled stuff; I believe most schools don't have a kitchen as such.

Mum did not cook anything very 'exotic'. We never had a curry or bolognaise. I thought I didn't like fish or mushrooms because Mum hated them and I never even tried them in my early years.

I loved bread and jam and would gorge myself on it whenever I could. Huge doorsteps, as we called thick cut slices, cut by hand I mean, not ready sliced bread. I also loved sweets and ate loads of them. My school satchel probably had more sweet wrappers in it than books!

Consequently, because I didn't brush my teeth enough, I suffered the most horrendous toothache and had many fillings with that silver-looking mercury amalgam stuff. My dentist didn't use an anaesthetic when he drilled, he was just really careful and he never seemed to strike a nerve! I also had many extractions and actually got to quite like the anaesthetic gas. They used to put this big black rubber mask over your nose and mouth and you breathed in the gas. It gave you some nice dreams I recall, but it didn't work that way for everyone.

I think that toothache is a worse pain than childbirth. There is currently a big problem of tooth decay in young children and dental experts are urging schools to be sugar free zones.

I have been a yoyo dieter in my day, tried most of them, Atkins, Scarsdale, low fat, no fat, fasting, diet pills, laxatives, bingeing and vomiting. I was fortunate not to get stuck in that one and get a full-blown eating disorder.

Once my husband and I went to the TT races on the Isle of Man which is one of the most exciting things you can do, if you like motorcycles. We saw Agostini outside our B&B as they garaged the MV Augusta nearby, The TT is highly dangerous and virtually every year a competitor or tourist is killed (Mike Hailwood the greatest TT rider ever, survived all his races only to be killed at 41 when a lorry hit his car, he was taking his kids to get fish and chips, that tragic irony is heart rending). Anyway, sorry I digress. We went for a week and I ate so much that I couldn't wear the same pair of trousers home that I had worn on the outward journey. I had to wear a pair of my husband's trousers. I think it was the coconut mushrooms that were largely to blame.

My weight has varied considerably over the years; when I hit the menopause, my energy just went and I stuffed my face and went up to 11.5 stone but I got through it without any other symptoms and then got my diet under control again.

I was an ovo-lacto vegetarian for 20 years and bought my children up as vegetarian for the first six years of their lives. After that, they would start trying meat when they went to friends' houses and ultimately announced that they did not want to be vegetarian anymore. I also resumed eating meat and fish again, although I knew that the human gut is not designed to process meat; it is too long and meat travels too slowly and can start to putrefy. Nowadays we have polluted the seas and fish are absorbing plastic particles and also many farmed fish carry diseases.

However, a vegetarian diet can leave one with low vitamin B 12 and phosphorous but a supplement can be taken. I am now a vegetarian again and also have a lot of vegan dishes which are delicious. However, I do really enjoy a fillet steak, but now I do not chew meat, I eschew meat! I stopped eating meat originally when I was influenced by my dear friend Barbara, back in the late 1960s. Ironic, even though my dad was a butcher (or because of it), I had never really thought of the suffering of animals. If you care to explore this subject, there is of course plenty of information online, some of it very graphic. For the sake of the planet, I think we should all be going into vegetarianism or veganism. Veganism is a way of living which seeks to exclude, as far as possible and practicable, all forms of exploitation of cruelty to animals for food, clothing or any other purpose. It has been called 'eating the rainbow' and more and more people are adopting veganism. There is a great vegetarian restaurant in Brighton, East Sussex called 'Terre a Terre'.

There wasn't much around in the late 1960s, when I had my consciousness raised about what I was consuming. It was pretty much Tofu or TVP (Textured Vegetable Protein). What am I saying?? I have a ready meals mind-set! There were always eggs, fruit, fresh vegetables, seeds and nuts. Vegetarianism was dismissed as a fad or mad. I remember reading an item about George Bernard Shaw, a pacifist and committed vegetarian.

He was in a restaurant and a fellow diner looked at his plate of food and enquired, "Are you going to eat that or have you just eaten it?"

Other noted vegetarians are Mark Twain, Voltaire, Plutarch, Pythagoras, Confucius and Tolstoy.

Tolstoy said, "When the suffering of another creature causes you to feel pain, do you submit to the initial desire to flee from the suffering one? On the contrary, come closer, as close as you can, to he who suffers and try to help him."

Einstein and Gandhi were also vegetarian and it was Leonardo da Vinci who said, "The day will come when men such as I will look upon the murder of animals as they now look upon the murder of men."

Then there is Cesar Chavez, Rosa Parks and Hitler – well if Hitler tried vegetarianism, he failed as he did in his other endeavours. In 1964, his personal chef Dione Lucas, listed turtle soup, stuffed pigeon and sausages amongst his favourite foods. Ruby Hamad, who reported the above and is a vegan, said simply that veganism is not a diet and its philosophy is this; do the least harm wherever possible, chose the option which causes the least suffering, the least environmental destruction and the least damage.

If you practice the true science of yoga, a vegetarian diet is one to follow and as your body, mind and energy become aligned or in union, there will be balance and inner calm.

Chapter 6: Sunday School, Church and God Stuff

I think I might go to my town centre and have a placard and some leaflets saying you are a miracle, a product of life itself, you are a drop of the divine as are we all, you come from the source of creation. The placard would also declare there is no God, only one of your own creation and we are in Heaven right here and now. Or I would have a sandwich board with **'Prepare to Meet Thy Doom'** on it; that would be apposite, because we are screwing up our Heaven on Earth.

Or I could go knocking on doors and deliver the message like the Jehovah Witnesses. When you practice love, empathy, expanded awareness, compassion, inclusivity and forgiveness, one wonders at the infinite potential there is for coming up with different doctrinal interpretations. The witnesses believe that the present world order is under the control of Satan and, if that is the case, I can think of some more wholesome remedies for the overcoming of that power, any mission that has a 'governing body' with no place for women should be viewed with some scepticism.

It is said that there is no difference between theists and atheists; they both believe something they don't know. As more people think for themselves, religions will crumble. I agree, when I see what has been happening to religious organisations in my lifetime. I think that belief is just an acronym for:

Blindly
Enduring
Life
In
Existential
Fear

My parents never went to church but they had me christened in one. I have a booklet with my christening photos and the church magazine, which included the announcement of my christening. They did send us to Sunday School, probably so that they could have a break. I loved hearing bible stories and the teachers had a board that felt shapes would adhere to, e.g. a palm tree, a camel or the good samaritan. One of the teachers had dirty hands; they always looked black and I later discovered that he was a local coal merchant..

We went to a church called the Congregational Church and I couldn't understand why there were so many different names, like Baptist, Presbyterian, Catholic etc. I thought that there was only supposed to be one God and one Bible, but there seemed to be so many spin-offs, it seems that people like to have their own version of the truth.

We had a vicar that I really liked, his name was Reverend Franks, he was kind and caring and I thought that Jesus would have liked him; he lived his faith which a lot of churchgoers didn't seem to do. I was persuaded to take the scripture exam and we had preparatory lessons with Reverend Franks. I got 96 marks and still only came third! I had to go to Brighton to collect my certificate at a special ceremony. Mum and Dad didn't come – going out to events seemed beyond them and we didn't have a car.

Eventually I joined the church choir and had choir practice on a Friday evening and then I attended two services on a Sunday. We had to wear a black cassock type garment with a detachable white-collar and I was always trying to pop a sweet into my mouth surreptitiously – not easy when you are sitting right at the front. I did enjoy it though, mostly we sang some lovely hymns and psalms and once we performed Handel's Messiah in a combined choir. The beautiful church was in town. It was called Steyne Gardens Methodist and it had a huge pipe organ; I think that it's a Coptic church now.

It's amazing how many churches have closed or are being used for other purposes. One of our smaller local churches, with a beautiful facade became a pub called 'Ten' (maybe from the Ten Commandments)! When it first opened, they had the audacity to put in a big statue of a naughty nun pulling up her habit to reveal a garter just above the knee – unbelievable. It seems to reflect the dwindling numbers of churchgoers, though I do not think that this means that people are not engaged in some form of spiritual practice.

I used to pray to God to forgive my misdemeanours, I even used to bargain with 'Him', e.g. I would pray that if I didn't refrain from masturbating, then something bad will happen; I never stuck to it and nothing bad really happened but it's strange bargaining with a supernatural being.

My brother lost his faith, such as it was, when he found a baby owl and tried to rear it. Peter prayed to God to let it live but it died and so did his faith.

Once we were all on our way to the Harvest Festival, just us three kids as Mum and Dad never came to church as I have said. We had tins of food and fresh produce from the garden. We were nearly at the church, when Peter said, 'I'm not going,' and he marched off with his cabbage and fed it to the horses that were in a field quite near to the church.

That just reminds me of all the fields and open spaces we had to play in, in those days. We were so fortunate as they have all gone now, all built on and kids have few places to roam in, even if they are let out of the house alone as we were. They can't run free, make camps in the bushes, climb trees or see the beautiful meadow which was near our house. There is the park but that is sterile and boring.

When I was 16, I got fed up with the choir. I wanted to go to the YPF (Young Peoples' Fellowship) on a Friday evening and find boys to kiss so I left saying I was studying for my 'O' Levels. True – but not the reason for leaving – another lie!

I have always been a seeker and I started to explore other ideas about spirituality and became more drawn to eastern philosophies. I was born 18 days after India gained independence and I've always thought that some of that energy went into me. Mind you, that was another screw up by the British, not the independence, but the way it was done.

Thinking about my darling brother Peter and his dismissal of theologies, I will tell you what happened to him. Peter was born in 1949, the middle child of the three Hoads. He was a beautiful looking boy but a bit wild – there is a photo of him in this book. Deborah and I used to fight with him and we were quite frightened of him at times. I've already told you about him stealing money from our lodger.

Once when we all came home from school before Mum and Dad got home from work, we locked him out of the house as we were afraid of him. He went around banging on all the windows wanting to be let in. Eventually he smashed one of the panes of glass in the French doors. We were all suddenly united in a common cause, i.e. how to explain this occurrence to Mum and Dad. I have also told you about the shed roof incident.

Peter began drinking alcohol at quite a young age and I guess was really an alcoholic or at least a binge drinker. Peter met his first wife when he was 18, who was four years older than him. She became pregnant and, as she was a Catholic, I think she didn't use contraception, but Peter did the 'right thing' and married her when he was 19. He was working for Walls the cooked meats company and he was a van boy doing deliveries. When he got married, he got his own round and moved to Eastbourne where he bought their first house; I think it only cost about 5,000. Our dad was very dubious saying he shouldn't be 'saddled with a mortgage'. I think it was amazing, it was 1969 and they had a beautiful daughter, but the relationship faltered and Peter, who was very attractive to women, was unfaithful. Eventually his wife left him, but they were later reconciled and they had a son in 1973. A lovely boy who grew up to have a natural acting talent. Sadly, after some years, they divorced.

Peter married again but there were a lot of complications due to her ex-husband and that marriage also ended in divorce.

My brother had worked for Philip Morris the tobacco company and retired early with a good pension. He had been visiting Goa with a group of good friends for a holiday for many years usually around December and January. Peter was famous for his drinking and many people in Colva knew him;

52

they nicknamed him 'A.M. Pete' and 'P.M. Pete', for obvious reasons, with the alcohol kicking in in the afternoon.

In early 2013, I had returned from Australia on a Monday in January and on the Wednesday, I got a phone call from Peter's second ex-wife Barbara to say he had died in his hotel room – he was 63. At that point, Peter and Barbara had reconciled and were just in the process of selling the house they both owned; Peter was living in it and she was living in a flat. They had put in an offer on a flat in Peacehaven and were going to live together again. The first thing Barbara and I had to do was go to the Indian Embassy in London to get an emergency visa, it was a cold snowy day as we travelled and the embassy staff were wonderful. The astonishing thing was that we were able to book a cheap flight to Goa with Monarch Airline on the train ride back from London, we used Barbara's little laptop. We therefore flew out a matter of days from first receiving the news!

Barbara and I had to go to Goa as Peter had died without seeing a doctor. The police had to be called and he was in the local mortuary. The owner of the hotel knew Peter very well, having hosted him and his friends for many years and he was really fond of Peter. The first thing Barbara and I had to do was be interviewed by the police to establish his identity, etc. We then had to go to the mortuary where the post-mortem would be carried out. It all looked very basic and somewhat primitive and one of the mortuary attendants was wearing a plastic apron with Disney characters on it! I couldn't look at his body, but Barbara did just to reassure herself that it was Peter.

The post-mortem revealed that he had contracted pneumonia and his liver was in a poor state. We then had to decide what to do with Peter's body as we could not take it back to the UK. Ultimately, we decided to have him cremated in the Hindu tradition and bring his ashes home.

The hotel owner was absolutely magnificent and arranged everything for us. He bought a new outfit for Peter to wear for his cremation and he actually dressed him – he did everything with such care and respect. Peter's body was put in the back of the funeral car which was like a little Bedford van and we followed it to the crematorium. His body was wrapped in a white sheet and we could see his feet in white socks sticking out through the clear back windows! The van driver got lost and we had to stop by a recreation ground and ask for directions from some people playing cricket.

Eventually we arrived at the crematorium in Panjin. I have photos of the site which is a huge consecrated open space with several sections in case there is more than one cremation happening (there was only one other when we were there). I also have photos of the cremation in case family members wished to see what happened. Peter's body was placed on the wood pyre and we put a flower on him and said some prayers.

His body was then covered in more wood and Barbara ignited the pyre. I stood for some hours, watching my brother's body burn – Barbara and another friend didn't watch and went for a coffee.

Interestingly, during the cremation process, the femur was forced up at a 90-degree angle due to the effect of the heat on the ligaments. Peter had attended a cremation himself after one of his friends died so he was familiar with the procedure. He had also helped smash up the bones of his friend as the heat was not intense enough to reduce them all to ashes. In fact, my brother remembered doing that for his friend and told us that he was cremated by a river in Goa and Peter couldn't smash up the pelvis, so he hurled it into the river. This may seem shocking and irreverent, but our society has sanitised death and kept hidden the realities of our mortality.

If you want to live life to the full, you need to be conscious of your own mortality as we are all heading for the grave, so live well now.

Incidentally, when one of Peter's friends saw the outfit, he had been dressed in for his funeral, he remarked that, "Peter wouldn't be seen dead in that tie!"

We had a wake at Peter's old watering hole, the Pevensey Bay Aqua Club where he had once been vice-commodore – he was a good and keen fisherman. We had most of our family there and so many of his friends. My daughter Jane, who had a business making novelty cakes, made a lovely one with a little fisherman sitting on it with a line into the water. Also, my darling sister Deborah had written a song about Peter, for those old enough to remember it – it was a pastiche of Terry Scott's song *My Brother* so sing along:

ODE TO PETER 'OAD (HOAD)

Who'll be remembered for his wry smile?
Who left this world and went out in style?
Who's gone to the heavenly pub in the sky?
Our brother
Who'd pass out on the kitchen floor?
Who'd get left by the old front door?
Who'd be the one to yell out for more?
Our brother
Who set fire to his green eiderdown,
After drinking it up one night in the town?
Who'd have stayed asleep while the house burned down?

Our brother

Our brother said it was not he, who put salt in Mr Ward's tea?

Our brother said that it was me

Our brother was rotten

Who broke his arm falling out of a tree?

And waited for a taxi lying on the settee?

Then missed his favourite programme on the TV?

Our brother

Who kept drinking despite his health?

Who put fishing above all else?

The love we have for him transcends everything else

Our brother

All joking apart, we miss our Pete

From the top of his head to the soles of his feet

He was a right little...but he was really sweet

Our brother

Who went to Goa and didn't come back?

To be with his mates and hang his last hat,

Who wouldn't be seen dead in a tie like that?

Our brother

Deborah and I sang that song to the gathered assembly at the wake; in the song, Deborah refers to Peter's drinking. He would sometimes pass out on the kitchen floor and once he didn't make it through the door and fell asleep on the garden path. Mr Ward was our old lodger. Once Deborah came home late and smelt smoke – Peter had been smoking and had fallen asleep. The eiderdown was smouldering and she doused it with water and put it out; he didn't even wake up! We must remember that death is a mystery and a certainty whatever your belief system.

All joking apart, this is a salutary tale and will also serve to remind people how precious life is and not to squander it for it is soon over. For my darling brother, over too soon.

Chapter 7: Sex and Boys

How about this for a double bind? It is said the so-called creator sets it up so that sex (intercourse) has to take place in order that you may exist, then tells you that you were born in original sin! Well anyway, that is what has been propagated by those who have a hotline to said creator.

Whoever wrote the Bible (which is really a history book written by people who were trying to make sense of humanity and the forces of nature) were of their time and ignorant. They got stuck when it came to Jesus and, as they had decided that having carnal knowledge of a woman was dirty, they had to invent the virgin birth to obviate the challenge of Him being born in original sin. There was so much begetting going on, I don't know why they had to focus on the natural process of reproduction as sinful when there were so many evils being perpetrated by those ancient tribes, e.g., wars, murder, mutilation and beatings. Even in these enlightened times, sex is still controversial, fraught with prejudice, censure, violence and judgement, particularly for women. Even menstruation is considered to be impure in some systems, or the butt of jokes or disgust. Again, it is another purely natural bodily function without which none of us would be around. Incidentally, I am reminded of the experience of Chad Varah, founder of the

Samaritans. In 1935 as an assistant curate, he conducted the funeral of a 14-year-old girl who had taken her own life as she had started menstruating and, being ignorant of her biology feared that she had a sexually transmitted disease, he became an advocate for sex education and a champion of the depressed and the suicidal.

Think of all of the euphemisms for menstruation; Aunt Flow, time of the month, on the rags, red tide/river/sea etc. Code Red, monthly visitor, Bloody Mary, shark week and 'having the painters in' to name but a few. An article in The Independent by Roisin O'Connor on 1st March 2016, claimed that a menstruation study found over 5000 slang terms for 'period' and euphemisms were found in ten different languages.

And what about sex between folk of the same gender? Don't go there because, according to those who claim to be the mouthpiece on earth of the Divine Creator, this is an abomination and, in some systems, they will kill you for it.

The whole creation is a miracle going back beyond four billion years and one bloke didn't do it! Will everyone please start thinking for themselves and question this robot mentality where information has been programmed into you, in some cases for thousands of years?

One human being has no right to judge another, even by claim to Divine diktat. We are all equal, though, as described by Orwell, some consider themselves to be more equal than others.

Surely it is time to let go of shame and guilt and be compassionate to one another, acknowledging that we are all a miracle – otherwise we are all screwed!

When I was at junior school, I had good friends who were boys, no sex involved, but they seemed to gravitate towards me. I think, with my mother as a role model, I was somewhat disparaging of their attentions. Thinking of *Great Expectations*, my mother was a lighter version of Miss Havisham and I was a lighter version of Estella. When I passed my 11 Plus exam, I could go to grammar school as opposed to the secondary modern school which was considered to be inferior as were the folk who attended it (a prime example of the damaging consequences of that system). I wanted to go to the Technical High School as it offered a more practical education, more suited to my limited academic capabilities. They even had animals, e.g. a calf and a goat, and taught some animal husbandry. It was a mixed school and just up the road from our house, easy to get to on my bicycle. However, my mother, having attended Varndean High School, wanted me to go to the High School for Girls; it was greater snob value and, in fairness, she probably thought it was the best school. I didn't have the knowledge or the guts to argue, so I was enrolled there and had to catch a train every day.

I had been so happy at my junior school, the teachers cared about us and our families and were so kind to us. My favourite teachers were Mr Groom and Miss Cook; when we left, Mr Groom put a quote from William Cowper in our autograph books: 'Knowledge is proud that he knows so much and Wisdom is humble that he knows no more.' Cowper was a poet and humanist (1731–1800) and was one of the most popular poets of his time. I'm glad that we got that brilliant quote and not a reference to one of his hymns, e.g. 'There is a fountain filled with blood drawn from Emmanuel's veins and

sinners plunged beneath that flood lose all their guilty stains.'
Reflect on that hymn while you are eating your Sunday lunch!

When you reach 11 years old, you are a senior in the junior
school and then you transition to the secondary school and
you are bottom of the pile. I absolutely hated it from day one
and was miserable for the next six years. I was out of my depth
and in the lowest set. The teachers were mostly dried up old
spinsters (I know; I am making my own feminist hackles
rise!). If you walked along the main dingy old corridor, you
could see old school photos going back for years. You know
the ones they take, where you could be in one end of the photo
and then run around the back and appear at the other end of
the photo as well. You could see a lot of the teachers in those
photos, probably from when they had just come out of
university and they had just stayed in the same school and
calcified.

We did have Biddy Burgum as a PE teacher who had
played hockey for England, and one male teacher called Mr
Du Feu, the French teacher. There was another PE teacher
who tried to teach us ballroom dancing; she wanted us to learn
because she asked how we were going to meet young men if
you can't ballroom dance! Whatever! The motto of the school
was 'The Utmost for the Highest' (I ask you!) and bugger all
for everyone else. One thing I did enjoy was acting, I would
still love to do some, whilst at school I played Bottom in *A
Midsummer Night's Dream* and did a comedy skit in the sixth
form revue. I also played the nurse in *Antigone* by Jean
Anouilh, not dreaming that I was to become one, I have a nice
press cutting for that one with a photograph.

Whilst I was there, they found an original tune for the
school song in a dusty old cupboard. That was another gem:

61

'Down where the Sussex Sea

Floats by caressingly

Warmed by the benediction of the sun

There fly our hearts and wills

As our lithe bodies fill

With vigour as we leap and dance and run.'

We had to learn the new/old tune so that we could sing this exquisite song!

Anyway, boys became an alien species – 'the other'. I found it more difficult to interact with them on a peer-to-peer basis and, of course, hormones were starting to kick in. I think that they manage the transition from junior to senior much better these days but I still loathe our education system as it teaches nothing much that is useful – like how to manage your body, mind and emotions or bring out one's individual gifts and talents. It just tries to cram you with information which seems of little consequence and puts you under enormous pressure to conform, perform and comply and to make you believe that passing exams is the measure of your worth. It feeds you into the economic engine, stunts your development and can cripple you emotionally.

Now art, music, fitness, exercise, nature study etc. are being squeezed out of the curriculum in favour of maths, English, science, IT, social studies, geography and history which we have never learned from; look at the state of the world!

Bearing in mind, we are in very turbulent times, politically, socially and globally and who got us into this shit? People who have been gifted a highly privileged education, e.g. those who attended Eton, Harrow, Oxbridge et al, so much for being highly educated. What they did learn in those hallowed halls was mostly selfishness, competition, elitism and naked ambition, instead of generosity, co-operation, inclusivity and social awareness.

If you can read and write, you can Google any information you need or you can just watch porn. Education should be a joyous, liberating experience but instead it is stressful, competitive and irrelevant as the planet burns. At least Greta Thunberg has seen the light.

Anyway, sex – I never got any sex education from my mother although she did ask me once regarding periods, 'You know what's going to happen when it happens don't you?' I said yes as, when we got to senior school, they gave us an information booklet entitled 'You're a Young Lady Now'. I ask you, laughable or not? I can still vividly recall the first time I touched a grown man's erect penis (I had a brother, so I touched his when we were kids). I think I was about 14 and my friend and I were going to the youth club and an 'older man' was giving us a lift, he was in his 20s. He was very tall, good looking and very softly spoken. Anyway, he and I were waiting for my friend in the corridor of the flats where she lived and he asked me if I had ever touched a man's penis, replying in the negative, I was then invited to do so and he unzipped his fly. I put my hand in and held his erection; I thought it was amazing and mysterious as it was hard, but the skin felt so smooth like silk or satin. It was a fascinating experience. I am not sure whether I touched the glans (not that I knew much about anatomy in those days) but I think it was just the shaft.

My mother never talked about sex, but she obviously had an impression of how it should happen, hence her guilt about my sister's conception which I mentioned earlier. I would have liked to have asked her some questions, e.g. did you ever have an orgasm? (So many women didn't achieve orgasm in those days and maybe that is still the case). I would also have liked to ask her if Daddy was any good in the sack.

Apropos the guy and his penis, I never really saw him again, he just gave us a lift to the club and that was that; I think his name was Les. In the early 1960s, you really did feel like a piece of meat and women were aware that they had something a man wanted – basically a hole with a person around it. A step up from a pound of liver in a jam jar! Incidentally, I once had a heated discussion with a client in a therapy group who maintained that 'a standing prick knows no conscience'! – I was being very unprofessional but couldn't believe what I was hearing. Anyway, at that time, you got groped, stared at, importuned and were the focus of lewd comments.

I was often embarrassed to wear sanitary towels which we did in those early days as we were told that you could not wear internal protection if you were a virgin. The towels were a great wedge of cotton wool around your crotch held up by a sanitary belt. I was worried that if someone groped me, they would get a handful of the pad! Beggars' belief! It is no better these days despite the laws on inappropriate touching.

I lost my virginity at age 15, standing up against a wall in an alleyway; he said it was just his finger but it wasn't. The guy involved was a sex addict and a serial molester of women; he must have hated us. I was besotted with him because I thought he was incredibly handsome with sort of Latin looks which I have always preferred. He kept pursuing me thereafter, I believe that he was proud that he was the first man to penetrate me. He ended up in prison for a sex offence, so at least some courageous woman had her day in court. Even then, I still corresponded with him whilst he was in prison. I don't think that he was in any way regretful of his behaviour.

I then began a long history of promiscuity fuelled by alcohol. I was a sexual predator; I would get drunk, pick up a beautiful man and do my own importuning. This behaviour escalated after my marriage failed. I got married when I was 21. I proposed on the rebound and we had a white wedding in a beautiful local church. I had met my future husband in one of the popular coffee bars at the time called the Waldorf Buttery. It was all coffee bars in those days. John would come in looking amazing in an ex-US Air Force sheepskin jacket. He wore a lot of army surplus stuff or Levi's shirts with a lot of dot snappers (press studs) and Levi's jeans of course. People were in awe of him, saying, 'Oh there's Johnny R.' He was engaged when I met him, but I was undaunted. John had a non-identical twin brother, Dave, and they were both keen on motorcycles (they were then the favoured mode of transport as most young men eschewed the closed environment of a car and the expense owning one incurred).

John's father had been killed in World War II and I think, partly because of that, he and his brother were intrigued by books on the war. John introduced me to the books of James Jones, e.g. *The Thin Red Line* and *From Here to Eternity*. I was stunned to read about the campaigns in Guam and Guadalcanal.

"I write about war," James Jones said, "because it is the only metier I've ever had."

Jones earned the purple heart after he was wounded in Guadalcanal. I couldn't believe that the soldiers used to drink Aqua Velva (an aftershave lotion with a high alcohol content) and orange juice. John also introduced me to science fiction writers such as Ray Bradbury and Theodore Sturgeon.

We were together for a year initially and used to meet up later in the evenings particularly Fridays after he had been drinking with his buddies who were a formidable crew. They used to drink bottles of cheap wine while sitting round the back of the local Lido facing the sea. One of John's friends, Martin, owned a Model A Ford and we used to go to Santa Pod raceway to watch him in the drag racing. It was a disused airfield, talk about a 'blasted heath', it was very barren and windy with few facilities and it's quite a smart venue now. Obviously, there were real dragsters there doing the quarter mile run which was really exciting. Martin won a trophy at one event. The US Army brought their drag car from a local base and we used to get good beer from them – Schlitz which I had never heard of – 'the beer that made Milwaukee famous'.

Thursday, March 18th, '65

Telephone Brighton 66799. Small ads 29244

The results of weeks and weeks of rehearsal will be seen tonight, tomorrow and Saturday evenings when the Girls' High School at Worthing put on their annual play. This year they are putting on the translated French tragedy, "Antigone," by Jean Anouilh. Antigone is played by 16-year-old Allison Neal (right). Pictured with her is 17-year-old Lindsay Hoad, who plays the nurse.

Newspaper Cutting

After a year, I ended the relationship and took up with the thieving, bodybuilding Borstal boy, whom I have already mentioned in the chapter on stealing. John wrote a heartfelt letter begging me to go back which I eventually did.

They say a wedding is for two people, the bride and her mother! Certainly, the case with me – Mum took over – she insisted on the church wedding and the boys had to wear top hat and tails (hired from Moss Bros) and she made the bridesmaids' dresses and her own hat. Mind you, Dad looked really great in his morning suit; he was always quite a dapper dresser and I think he loved it. I was late for the ceremony and, when I walked down the aisle and saw my intended in his suit, I hardly recognised him as he had had his long hair cut off.

I remember thinking to myself, who the hell is doing this? It wasn't me! We went to Paris for our honeymoon where we saw the aftermath of the student riots (I had visited the same area in Paris a couple of years earlier but more about that in a future chapter).

Being married didn't suit me, although I did use the time to do my 'A' Level English by correspondence course. My attitude to marriage puts me in mind of E.M. Forster who chose a quote from Shelley as the title of his novel *The Longest Journey*:

'I never was attached to that great sect whose doctrine is that each one should select out of the crowd a mistress or a friend and all the rest, though fair and wise, commend to cold oblivion. Though it is in the code of modern morals, and the beaten road Which those poor slaves with weary footsteps tread who travel to their home among the dead by the broad highway of the world, and so with one chained friend, perhaps a jealous foe, the dreariest and the longest journey go.'

Extract from *Epipsychidion*, by Percy Bysshe Shelley (1792–1822):

Epi – upon Psychidion – soul from the Greek

After three years, I left my husband and, strangely enough as I write this, today 14th September is my 51st wedding anniversary as we never got divorced. John is a dear friend and confidante and a sweet soul – we still see each other from time to time.

As I said, my promiscuity continued, and I was always looking for a meaningful overnight relationship.

I used to say: "I have had my share of men – and somebody else's!" I also said, "Why make one man miserable, when you can make fifty men happy?"

I did not particularly enjoy intercourse; I preferred to masturbate and create my own mind-blowing orgasm. What I did relish was the privilege of having a beautiful man's body under my hands. Sometimes it was like a sacrament, a form of worship. I loved kissing and using my tongue and exploring all of the erogenous zones. I think I was quite accomplished and I don't think any man was harmed in my pursuit of a one-night stand and the dismantling of my reputation.

Actually, that is patently untrue – I had a one-night stand in Kos (sex on the beach and it wasn't the cocktail) with a Greek chap and brought home a souvenir – colloquially 'a dose of the clap'. I shared it with my then boyfriend – he still speaks to me! Gonorrhoea, one of the oldest sexually transmitted diseases. I was lucky that that was it all it was. In those days the 'clap clinic' was just a part of the outpatient department and, as you sat there in shame and humiliation, they gave you a number to protect your anonymity. But when they called it out, everyone knew why you were there! These clinics are brilliant now, completely separate and the staff are wonderful. I think I had 2g of penicillin and that was it.

I was unfaithful to my husband and he was hurt but, as I said, we remain married and friends. Neither of us wished to re-marry, in my case, as stated earlier, marriage never suited me. I prefer to be alone. I marvel at people who can live together for decades but I want my own bed, my own stuff, my own books and my own room. I want to live life at my own pace and not answer to anyone and I don't want to disappear. My take on it is also summed up in that seminal work by Mike Naismith: *Different Drum* sung by Linda Ronstadt and the Stone Poneys. Oh, by the way, I'll be a post-feminist in post patriarchy.

I'm writing this in a hotel room at the Avisford Park Hilton; it is a glorious place and the staff are wonderful. I just went for a walk in the grounds which are really extensive and where there are the most mature stunning trees which appear to be well over 100 years old. One cedar is my particular favourite and you wouldn't believe how it has branched out (you can see it on the front cover of this book) and I often go and hug it. The wind was causing the leaves to rustle in some of the deciduous trees, whilst the cedar tends to stay silent in its majesty. I love the sound of the leaves, it seems each tree has a different note depending on the type of leaf, mesmerising. As Sadhguru would say, that is half your lungs out there. He has initiated the Green Hands Project in Tamil Nadu which is trying to save the soil which has become degraded because of deforestation. So far, they have planted over 45 million trees, check it out and donate if you can.

As far as sex goes, I haven't had intercourse for over a decade and I just don't feel the urge anymore, I do miss kissing though. I suppose it happens with age but not necessarily as a lot of older folks enjoy an active sex life.

They say (don't know who they are) you don't have to avoid temptation because ultimately temptation will avoid you! I am glad I didn't get stuck in this one, I could be schlepping around foreign parts finding young men who will service an old dear for a free dinner and a fake Rolex. Whatever floats your boat! When you practice yoga consciously, in my experience, you find yourself luxuriating in your whole body, rather than tweaking some nerve endings in your genitalia.

The second man I lived with was called Robin, and we worked in the same hospital and he was, and still is, a very skilled operating department technician. I think it was the first time I was courted, and he was a romantic who loved poetry, literature and music of all kinds. Once we went to Chichester Cathedral to listen to a performance of Pachelbel's Canon in 'D', and another time we went to London to see The Sex Pistols, but it was just too crowded to get in. Anyway, it felt strange to be chosen as I usually like to do the choosing.

Robin took me to Thomas Hardy's cottage, we also visited the village of Slad and I sat in the pub chair once used by Laurie Lee. He read me *P. Smith, Journalist* by P.G. Wodehouse when we stayed together in the on-call room at the hospital, although I wasn't supposed to be there. He could be called out at any time in the night to assist when emergency surgery was required; it could be anything from road traffic accidents to Caesarean sections.

Robin organised a lovely flat to live in and we entertained a lot. I was fortunate to meet his friends who were all accomplished and wonderful people. One of them, Richard, lived in France and we went to stay with him and his girlfriend. I didn't even know anyone who could speak French prior to that! Robin was very beautiful and had a courtly manner. He was an absolute firebrand when it came to political discussions, arguing for his Socialist principles. Once we had to leave his parents' house because he got into a highly volatile conversation with an uncle from South Africa when apartheid was still the functioning system. I feel Robin raised my awareness in social and cultural matters as he had high standards.

He was a great lover, but our relationship only lasted about three years and then he had to leave me as I was becoming impossible to live with. My RMN training came in those three years and it made a deep impact on me, not always in a good way. He actually came to London with me and got a job at St Bartholomew's Hospital (a renowned teaching hospital), when I was doing my training at the Maudsley Hospital and secretly stayed with me in the nurses' accommodation.

I still see Robin from time to time and we are good mates. In fact, I saw him recently and he was intrigued that I was writing a book and wondered what I would say about him, well now he knows!

The next chap I lived with (briefly) was called Sam or Sami – he was a Ugandan Asian who had come to England when General Idi Amin caused his family to leave Uganda. Amin had a colourful sobriquet; he was known as 'The Butcher of Uganda' and had served in the British Army in the King's African Rifles from 1946–1962. Human rights groups estimate that 100,000 to 500,000 people were killed under his regime, so Sam was lucky to get out alive. Amin was a formidable rugby forward, although one officer apparently said of him, 'Idi Amin is a splendid type and a good player but virtually bone from the neck up, and needs things explained to him in words of one letter' (Wikipedia).

My relationship with Sam didn't last long, although I tried hard to please him, really getting into Asian cooking and I got pretty good at chapatis. I think he felt uncomfortable with my past and my outspokenness as a woman and there was also a bit of a cultural clash.

From about 1981–1984,I lived with dear Tim, a very complex and anxious soul, but a great bon viveur. He was apparently born into a troubled family and was put up for adoption. His adoptive mother was a very conservative woman, almost Victorian in her outlook, and Tim was never very close to her. His father was an insurance agent and he lived in a fabulous detached house when I met him. Tim was sent off to public school when he was eight years old and it ruined him; one of his fellow students killed himself when he was 12 by jumping out of a window. However, Tim ended up with impeccable manners and a wonderful speaking voice, but also some traits of obsessive-compulsive disorder and chronic social anxiety. In the matter of lying, he had a PhD, and was a congenital liar.

He came to my flat one night and never moved out for three years! He never worked, saying he had independent means. What he actually did was lie to his mother to get her money, he told her he was studying accountancy in London, or that he was fighting a court case and never told her he was living with me. We did have a fun time though, mostly going to pubs and out for meals. However, after three years, when I was working full-time and doing two nights in a nursing home on a Friday and Saturday, I had had enough. I met Ashley and asked Tim to leave. This was just around the time I did the

EST training and, in the spirit of 'cleaning up' my life, I went around to see Tim's mother. At first, she wouldn't let me in the house and was quite abusive, but eventually she did let me in. She was horrified to hear the truth of his three years with me and showed me a list of all the sums of money she had given him. The house, though lovely, reeked of damp and she had all Tim's old shoes lined up in the conservatory stuffed with newspaper. She even still put a hot water bottle in his bed at night. She never had a television or a holiday and used to drink the cabbage water after she had cooked cabbage. Tim's dad died when he was 12 and it affected him deeply.

I pursued my affair with Ashley and eventually became pregnant with twins. That was a shock! I was 37 and so went for an amniocentesis test at 16 weeks, when I also had a scan and was told I was having twins; it had never entered my head that I would have more than one child. Strangely enough, Ashley was in the hospital on that day, having a bad tooth abscess drained. I went to the ward to give him the news and suffice to say, he was not best pleased!

I sold my flat and moved in with my mother and we bought her council house. My beautiful daughters were born six weeks early and I had to have forceps but refused any drugs. They weighed 4lb 2 oz and 3lb 12 oz when they were born, and the next day we had to go to a wonderful neo-natal intensive care unit in Brighton as my youngest daughter had trouble with her lungs. I tried desperately to bring my milk in with a breast pump but only ever got a few millilitres. Various factors were against me; my mother had died a month before the girls were born, I was what they called an elderly primigravida, and I had an infection. Blessedly, my daughters did well and I brought them home when they were six weeks old.

The naming of a child seems to ignite all sorts of dilemmas (look at the controversy over names when a new 'Royal' is born). I was in the doctor's waiting room, there for an ante-natal appointment when another patient came into reception. She gave her name as Lucy something and I immediately knew that that was a name I wanted; it comes from the Latin Lucius – Bringer of Light. Lucy is my firstborn and 15 minutes later, Jane arrived and I named her after my beloved cousin Jayne with whom I shared all sorts of adventures in my teens. Jayne has had many health problems in recent years and has borne them with incredible stoicism, courage and a joyful heart. She is an amazing woman and I love her very much.

My dearest friend Aileen visited me in the hospital and gave me her camera, so I had a picture of myself holding both the girls for the first time they came out of the incubator. In a lucky coincidence, there happened to be a young woman on the unit whom I had nursed when I was doing my SRN training and then, years later, when I worked in the day hospital. Her name was Susan and her husband was an accomplished photographer, so I have some brilliant pictures of my daughters in their incubators. Susan's daughter had been born at 28 weeks and she did well; it is amazing what can be done for premature babies now and this was 34 years ago.

My sister had left her husband and she moved into our house with her 13-year-old son. Deborah was amazing, having sorted out the house after Mummy died, she went to remove Mum's bed and discovered that the mattress had virtually rotted away, and springs were showing so Mummy must have slept on the same mattress for decades. It was such a sad and pitiful thought and we didn't realise what she had endured.

I returned to work initially part time when my daughters were three months old and Deborah was a great boon to us. After a year, Tim came back into my life and he became a surrogate father to the girls. I worked full time and he ran the house and brought them up. He was absolutely amazing in that role and the house was really tidy and the girls had a wonderful routine; he loved them so much and they him. Our relationship was rocky however and, after about six years, he moved out and I had various au pairs to look after the girls. Tim got his own flat at his mother's expense and he had the girls every other weekend, which was an absolute life saver for me. We were so blessed to have Tim. He was a loving stepdad and it gave him a reason to be. He couldn't drive and I bought a tricycle with two seats on the back and he went everywhere on it – they were quite a sight to behold.

Tragically, Tim became very ill when the girls were 17, he had not told anyone and was not even registered with a doctor. If it wasn't for my eldest daughter Lucy, who was particularly close to him, he probably would have just died alone in his bed. Eventually after Lucy's persistent begging, a doctor was called and he was admitted to hospital immediately. I had not seen Tim for a few months and I was deeply shocked to see him. He was wasting away with liver cancer and I knew from my nurse training that he was terminally ill. I thought he would only last about a week and sadly I was right. The girls and I spent hours with him in the hospital massaging his legs and feet and generally pouring all our love into him. He was put through all sorts of tests, which were patently futile, and I argued with his doctor about it. I was determined that he would not die in hospital and we managed to get him discharged to our flat which we set up with an adjustable bed and a recliner chair. Tim came home to us on a Friday afternoon and died the following day with his beloved Lucy beside him in the room. I confirmed his passing and all three of us lit a candle and spent a few minutes alone with him to say our last goodbyes.

The chaps from our funeral director were very sweet when they came to collect him, saying send him light and love. There is nothing sacred about the practical aspects of moving a dead body; Tim was 6ft and the chaps had to get him into a body bag and then negotiate two doorways and a corridor to take him out of the flat. In Hindu philosophy, there is a belief that there are five stages of death and we think it's over in an instant.

My girls had a great upbringing because of our beloved Tim, as I was a chaotic but diligent mother in the sense that I worked hard and tried to give my daughters everything they wanted. His funeral was a strange affair, his mother having died the year before and I had no knowledge of any of his relatives – sadly his very best friend, another Tim, couldn't be present as he was in China but the chapel was packed with my friends and family. My sister and brother-in-law Atholl came over from Australia to be with us and Deborah helped me clear out Tim's property which was a huge job (there is a whole other story here about Atholl and his mother, but that is his story to tell, bless his loving heart).

The vicar was one of those who tried to be funny and cool and failed miserably. My sister wanted to punch him in the face for his attitude and for calling Tim 'our friend' rather than the most precious stepfather to the children although I guess that it was my responsibility to convey how much he had contributed to our lives, but I obviously did not achieve that.

At one point, an amazing shaft of sunlight flooded in through the skylight, right onto my dear friend Aileen and the vicar said, "Oh the sun shines on the righteous."

He wasn't wrong as far as Aileen is concerned, however, it was almost as if he was implying that there wasn't much righteousness anywhere else – maybe that is unfair, but why say it? I think he may have been judgmental about our untypical family situation.

We held the wake in a hotel in Findon, a lovely venue and, strangely enough, the place of our first proper date.

On that first date, I remember that Tim asked me, "What made you become a nurse?"

I was trying to be enigmatic so I jokingly replied, "I like watching people suffer."

Well, I've certainly done a lot of that! Actually, I didn't like seeing people suffer but, ever since my childhood, I think I had an antenna out for suffering. I was so attuned to it after watching my parents for years who always seemed to be suffering life. Consequently, I have always felt impelled to intervene to try and alleviate suffering as though it was my job – I still behave like a rescuer at times. This book is partly written to help people wake up to reality, or urge them, as Rumi said, to 'be like a tree, let the dead leaves drop'.

I still have Tim's ashes in a casket and I also have his mother's ashes as he never dealt with them, in fact the funeral director still had them! Fortunately, we used the same director he'd had for his mum!

The last chap I lived with was a brother of a friend of mine and I was besotted with him. I'm not quite sure what it was but I just felt so at ease in his company. He had a very down to earth attitude and we had a passionate few weeks together before he had to go abroad for work. I wrote letters to him extolling his virtues and our relationship. Sadly, he never got the letters as he worked in Nigeria. I remember receiving his first letter to me and I literally fell to my knees in abject misery and shock. He dismissed what had passed between us as though it was just a fling and he did not recognise how I had felt about him. I think he knew of my history and just didn't trust me – can't say I blame him. Anyway, when he returned home, we resumed our relationship and eventually I sold my house and moved in with him.

However, it all went wrong from day one. I couldn't stand the way he just grunted in the morning, thinking it was amusing. He also didn't like my domestic skills including my cooking and he didn't much care for my children whom he called 'rug rats'. I don't really count this as living with someone – I think I was more of a lodger. After a little while, I moved out of his bedroom and spent six months sleeping in a sleeping bag on the floor of his box room; there was just enough space. He was even concerned that I may try to make a claim on his property – which was absolutely ridiculous! After the six months of purgatory, I moved out with the girls and got my own place – we didn't keep in touch.

MEA CULPA

Having just written about my sexual exploits and admitting that I haven't had intercourse for over a decade, I recently went out to a local pub to meet up with friends and listen to a live band. Writing this book has been an emotional roller coaster and I was feeling light-headed – I had been avoiding alcohol since embarking on the Isha Yoga programmes but that night I had some prosecco and then some more prosecco.

I was approached by a young chap – well he was 21! He was dancing with me and we kissed. The whole episode was crazy but I was having fun and he urged me to go back to his place where we enjoyed some rather athletic sex and I left in the early hours of the following morning. I had such a good time and was not going to succumb to sexual guilt. I didn't realise it was 'Grab a Granny' night!

Apropos my previous entry, I was intrigued to know what message I would receive from Sadhguru the following morning. When you join the Isha Foundation you have access to the hugely generous offerings from Sadhguru online; you can have access to so much of his wisdom and teachings online for free without joining. I signed up to receive a quote from Sadhguru every morning, it is called Wake Up to Wisdom. So, the following morning following my liaison with the lovely 21-year-old, this was it:

'Unless you do the right things, right things will not happen to you'. His talk was entitled *Do the Right Thing* – "If the right things aren't happening to you, don't blame the stars," Sadhguru says, "you simply have to do the right things."

In the body of his talk for the morning after the night before, he further says: "It is because people are unable to bear the torture of the mind that they have devised many ways in society to go below the mind. Excessive eating, alcohol, and excessive indulgence in physical pleasures; these are all ways to go below the mind. People use them and for a few moments they forget the torture. You hit the bottle and sleep, for a few hours your mind does not bother you anymore because you have gone below the mind. There is great pleasure and it is so relaxing because suddenly the tortures of your mind are not there, so you get deeply addicted to it. If, by using a chemical, you go below the mind you will see life always catches up with you with more intensity after it is over. It is always so; suffering intensifies. The process of yoga is to see how to go beyond the mind, only when you are beyond the mind, can you really be yourself."

In the same offering for that morning, Sadhguru addresses a question about how you know if you are progressing on the Spiritual Path.

He says, "If you can still laugh and joke when things aren't going so well, that is progress and the fewer conditions you put on this life, that is progress."

Well, I was smiling, thank you, Sadhguru, it was almost like he knew what I was up to! I have been disciplined in my yoga practice since finding Sadhguru and doing the Inner Engineering course.

That last evening, I had slipped right back into the old pattern after over a decade, well 12 years as the last encounter had been on the night of my 60th birthday with an 'old flame' who came to my party. It was such a salutary lesson of how vigilant one must be when following a spiritual path.

Pranam and Blessings, my dear, Sadhguru.

Chapter 8: Risk Taking

Risk – a situation involving exposure to danger

> *'Risk is the consequence of the activities and*
> *associated uncertainties.'*
>
> (Tery Aren, Professor)

That's life, isn't it? Here are some of my risk-taking highlights. When I was about 17 and still at school, my friend Annita and I were in a holiday romance with two guys who were studying at The Sorbonne. One was a local chap whom my friend was seeing and I was with his friend, Chad, an American boy who had come to Worthing for his holiday. They returned to Paris after their break and left us with an address. We decided to go and visit them; I lied to my parents and said that I was going on holiday with a friend and her family – they didn't even check it out! We got visitors' passports – in those days, you could get one from your local main post office. They looked like a birthday card with your photograph on them and they were valid for a year. My friend told her family that she was leaving home. We had very little money and I can't remember how we arranged it all but anyway we booked the night ferry to Dunkerque. We took a train to London and had some time to kill so went to the Victoria Palace Hotel for a show. I think it was something hideous like 'The Black and White Minstrels' – can you Adam and Eve it?

We landed in Dunkerque (Dunkirk) and we were not sure how to proceed because we were originally going to hitchhike to Paris but someone suggested it would be better to hitchhike to Brussels and then on to Paris which is what we did. We got into vans, cars and lorries with random drivers, all male, and everyone was very kind to us. When we got to Brussels, we asked for directions from a uniformed chap whom we thought may be a policeman but turned out to be a postman! Anyway, he was a good pick for asking directions and we eventually hitchhiked to gay Paris. We went to the address the guys had given us only to find it was a Post Restante – just a place where they picked up their mail. Fortunately, it did have connections to the university and there were students around. We just looked at each other in disbelief – what to do? We saw one student who looked friendly and approached him to see if he knew Chad and Chris and he didn't, although he did suggest that if we went to a certain bar in the evening, they were likely to be there as it was a popular venue for students to hang out.

Talk about the kindness of strangers, he was American and he took us in his car and we saw some of the Paris sights like L'Arc de Triomphe, Jardin de Tuileries and Notre Dame. He bought us some bread and cheese and stayed with us until evening and then took us to the bar he had mentioned. Astonishingly, Chris and Chad were there! Although they were not pleased to see us – it has to be said that we were just a holiday diversion for casual sex really. However, they were kind enough to let us stay at their lodgings, which was risky as they were fearful of the landlady finding us, as they were not permitted to have guests.

My friend did not want to go home and decided to look for a job, whereas I was still at school. So, the next day we went to a café which was right near Pont Notre Dame and we could see the (now blighted) cathedral. I think it may have been the Petit Pont on Rue du Petit Pont – it was near the Latin quarter anyway.

At that time Paris was teeming with young people and a lot of them were sleeping under the bridges of the Seine; it was a time of restlessness and tumult amongst young Europeans. I was to return to that area in September 1968 on my honeymoon and there was a huge police presence as there had been the student riots in May 1968. You could see where the cobbles had been torn up to use as missiles against the police. It had continued for about a month and at one point seemed to trigger a one-day strike and demonstration on 13th May, called by the major union federations, who had their own grievances, and were appalled by the police brutality towards the students.

Eventually workers were demonstrating across France suggesting that De Gaulle should go. Students had occupied the Sorbonne, which police re-took on16th June.

Daniel Cohn-Bendit was a French student leader and activist who told demonstrators, "Nobody is responsible for you, you are responsible for yourselves."

The 1960s saw an awakening of existential angst; Jean Paul Sartre, the French Existentialist, claimed that man has nothing to cling to because God did not exist. His partner, Simone de Beauvoir, with whom he had an open relationship for 51 years, had written what I consider to be one of the most astounding works of feminist literature, *The Second Sex,* which inspired some further great feminist writers like Kate Millet, Betty Friedan and Germaine Greer, so there was a feminist wave as well in the 1960s. De Gaulle called an election for 23rd June and won a massive victory – it was another establishment coup and the revolutionary fervour dissipated.

Back to the cafe! My friend started chatting with an American girl who was selling newspapers outside L'Opera to get some money and they went off together as this girl thought she might know of a family who wanted an English au pair. I was left sitting outside at the cafe table, with no money and nowhere to stay. Eventually I was approached by a chap, I guess he was in his 40s, who introduced himself as Michael, an Armenian photojournalist. He bought me a coffee and we talked about his work and later he invited me for dinner at a Moroccan restaurant. We had the most amazing couscous with chicken and vegetables. I got completely pissed on red wine and ended up going back to his hotel room and passing out.

I woke up about 4:30 a.m. and found I was lying next to him; he was incredibly hirsute with thick black hair all over his back and chest. I got up rapidly and then sat by the window for a few hours until he woke up. He was a very sweet guy and he took me to the only Armenian printing press in Paris as he had to see his friend – he seemed a bit disillusioned with life and felt he needed inspiration. I was so fortunate that he had not tried to force any sexual attention on me. We returned to the cafe and amazingly Annita turned up, needless to say she hadn't found a job – I'm not sure what she did that night.

I saw her recently and we are still friends and have known each other since 1964.

Michael took us to the British Consulate/Embassy, not sure which, where we told an official our tale of woe and teenage indiscretions i.e. 'We came on holiday by mistake' a la Withnail and I. Our passports were taken and we were given a travel warrant with ID and some money and then we were repatriated. There were a lot of young people getting repatriated from Paris to various European countries as Paris was and is often a magnet for artists, socialists and random thrill seekers. We came back on the ferry and then took a coach to Victoria Bus Station and we had just enough money for a sandwich before we boarded the coach for Worthing. I got home saying I had had a lovely holiday in Paris with my imaginary friend and her family whereas Annita was disowned by her parents and had to go and stay with relatives. A few weeks later, I got a letter from the Foreign Office requesting payment of the £9 they had given me which was the cost of returning me to the motherland. Talking about mothers, she didn't enquire further about the communication from the Foreign Office so I must have concocted some story at the time. Dad was always on the periphery of our family unit and I think that the byword for all our exploits was: 'Don't tell your father.' I think in those days, many fathers were distant. Actually I think that they were distanced by their families who didn't want to risk incurring their wrath.

When I was 25, and doing my SRN training, I had a good friend in my set called Susan, she was from Coventry. Unlike me, she was very principled, responsible, conservative and sensible and I was amazed at her maturity; one evening I went into the nurses' sitting room and she was talking with an insurance broker about life insurance! We once went on holiday together to Tenerife, my first real holiday abroad (I didn't enjoy my honeymoon); both trips to Paris were by ferry so it was my first flight.

Bull Fighting the baby bull in Tenerife

One evening, we went to a nightclub/restaurant and had a lot of champagne – there is a lovely champagne area in Tenerife! Haha! There was an announcement that patrons had an opportunity to fight a baby bull, a small one for the women and a larger one for the men. Susan and I were the only women to volunteer and out the back of the nightclub was a really fair-sized bull ring – you can see it in the photograph.

We had to enter the ring and hold a really heavy canvas cape for protection; we were also accompanied by a chap who stood with us for protection. I think I went first, and it was quite an experience, but I was somewhat inebriated so I was fearless. When they released the bull, I didn't think that it looked very babyish and I think that the guy who was helping me looked more frightened that I did. I bet they are not allowed to do such a stunt nowadays – everything has become sanitised and we have health and safety up the whazoo.

Another thing I did which was quite risky happened in the United States. I went to Connecticut for the Co-Counselling International (a five day residential event). A few of us including my sister went into New Hampshire and climbed Mount Monadnock at night; luckily there was a full moon. The elevation is 3,165ft above sea level. I was wearing plimsolls and socks for gloves – it was somewhat foolhardy, but I almost made it to the top. My sister made it all the way, but some people had to give up because they were freezing. I must have had a good cardiovascular system in those days as I was toasty warm with the climb. We stood and watched the sunrise and then made our descent for pancakes and maple syrup at a local diner.

Another time, when my children were ten weeks old, I took them to Glastonbury festival. My dear friend Cathy travelled down with me and her husband and others in our party had travelled down separately and we were supposed to meet them. My poor girls had to put up with bottles of cold formula as we had no way of warming them. We drove onto the site and it was like the Somme; everyone was knee deep in muddy water. We couldn't find our gang, so we left a note on the communal bulletin board and drove into Netherstowey and stayed with our friend Christine.

Me and my kids

Again, when my kids were four years old, I took them to an Ashram about 50 miles outside Bombay. It was 1989 and we were to stay for three weeks which included the Christmas holiday. It wasn't easy managing two young children on the flights, as I was alone with them; they wanted to run up and down the aisle of the plane and also, we had to change flights in Istanbul. When we got to Bombay (now Mumbai), I was absolutely stunned by the traffic noise, the seething mass of humanity and the beggars, including women with their babies, in the gutters.

I didn't know what I was doing so we just got into a taxi that looked quite sound – the driver was very proud of his 'luxury' vehicle. The first thing he did was buy some paan, a preparation combining betel leaf with areca nut which is chewed for its stimulant and psychoactive effects, then it is either swallowed or spat out. Anyway, after an amazing journey past slum dwellings, people defecating on the roadside, random cows roaming free and of course crazy traffic with the diesel trucks blaring their horns, we finally arrived safely at the Ashram. It seems that the Indians have no concept of the rules of the road and it is every man for himself, so sadly there are a lot of casualties – fortunately we were not amongst them.

The Ashram was absolutely stunning, fashioned over decades by devotees out of what was forest and we had a great but quite challenging time there.

Being the sixties, I also took the risk of trying out recreational drugs, in those days we saw drug use as a way of raising our consciousness or enhancing our consciousness, not just getting 'out of it'. I tried LSD a few times and had some profound experiences as I did it with trusted friends in a safe environment. I also smoked cannabis and took amphetamines, the former made me feel paranoid and the latter was incredible in that it made me feel full of joy and love – until the come down. I was very fortunate that I didn't become addicted and I had friends who sadly did so and some who died as a result. When I started practising meditation, I realised that joy is a natural experience and there is no need for synthetic highs.

Weekend hippies, Newport Pagnell service station

There are always risks in life but the biggest one is that you will risk drawing your last breath and realise that you never really showed up in your own life.

I am reminded of a quote by Edwin Elliot – I think he was a mathematician – 'By being yourself, you put something wonderful in the world that was not there before.'

I guess the risk I have taken lately is writing this book, if it gets published will it be something wonderful?

Chapter 9: Sport, Exercise, Ballet and Yoga

I wasn't a great one for sport and not great at athletics but, having said that, I was captain of the rounders team at my junior school; I was really good at throwing the ball long distances so I was good at fielding. I loved cricket because my dad played it and, one year, I played in an inter-youth club tournament over in Hove. I bowled and fielded and got three wickets that day; there happened to be a spotter for the Sussex Ladies Cricket Team watching and they invited me to go for a trial, but I didn't take them up on the offer. There was a write up in the local gazette where it was mentioned that I had the offer from the Sussex Ladies, but I have lost the newspaper cutting. This is an example of missed opportunities and talent wasted. When I got to the high school, I hated netball and hockey, the latter being bloody dangerous. As I mentioned earlier, we had Biddy Burgum as a PE teacher so hockey was promoted.

Sadhguru has said that when you join in a game, say football or cricket, you become fully involved, many things leave your mind and your focus is on the ball. Of course, golf is very frustrating, it is the only game where the ball is not moving when you address it! We need to be fully involved in the game of our life.

In the summer months, I opted for javelin because you could mess about in the far corner of the sports field and the teacher didn't usually bother you. I wasn't any good at that either. One of the events at sports day was throwing the rounders ball and one year I won it, and then held the record for some time afterwards. I threw the ball 189' 7inches whatever that is in metres. I'm not sure how long that record stood.

I got a lot of points for the school house I was in which was Atalanta, her of the golden apples. In Greek mythology, she was a renowned and swift footed huntress, who was unwilling to marry, but offered to marry any man who could outrun her. Nobody could and those she overtook, she speared. Hippomenes wanted her and prayed to Aphrodite, she gave him three of the golden apples of the Hesperides which he dropped along the path. Atalanta stopped to pick them up and lost the race. Not the first or last woman to be tricked with a bit of gold.

I never really did much exercising as such although sometimes I did a bit of a workout. I did at one point do quite a regular workout with the Beverley Callard video which I think is really a good one, I couldn't cope with Jane Fonda 'going for the burn'. When I was about four, Mum enrolled me in a ballet class, in fact all three of us went to ballet but my brother soon dropped out. I went as far as Grade five, passing the exams, but I couldn't do block work as I had bunions even at that age. I was in a lot of local music festivals doing character work mostly, like the little match girl or the sailor's hornpipe. I did enjoy it but I wasn't really a very good dancer, unlike my sister Deborah who was absolutely brilliant. She went all the way to Elementary and Advanced and had an audition at the Royal Ballet when she was about 14; sadly she was unsuccessful and it broke her for a while as she believed it was what she was meant to do. I didn't fully understand this until years later; I'm sure if we'd had money or pushy parents, she would have got in, if not the Royal Ballet, then into another company – but that was it. Anyway, you don't have to go to a school to be a dancer and she is a natural born dancer and always will be. We would dance at every opportunity when she and I went to local nightclubs like The Scoobidoo or The Mexican Hat; we'd dance for hours to the great music of the time, Wilson Pickett, The Isley Brothers, Marvin Gaye, The Four Tops, Aretha Franklin and all the other great soul singers. Just listen to them 50 years later – they are absolutely amazing. Some people could actually stay sitting down while these records were playing!

Yoga

Sadhguru says, "How do you access the non-physical aspects of your life energy?"

The yogic practices which involve postures, breath, attitudes of mind and energy activation are all essentially orientated towards aligning the first three layers of the body, the physical, the mental and the energetic body. It is only in aligning them that you find access to dimensions beyond the physical – to the fundamental life energy itself.'

I started doing yoga in the mid-1960s in front of the television with Richard Hittleman who presented a programme called *Yoga for Health*. I have practiced it with various levels of discipline for many years and also did some classes; a friend of mine opened a yoga centre in Worthing which is still open today. She is a wonderful teacher who was taught by B.K.S Iyengar himself and she also taught in San Diego.

I have been blessed with a flexible frame and fortunately have managed to maintain that flexibility, not that it is necessarily the key to good yoga practice.

Really, I didn't start practicing yoga correctly until I encountered Sadhguru and was initiated into the kriyas. I have been doing Hatha yoga and Iyengar yoga for many years every day as I am capable of some self-discipline. I used to brag that I did a headstand every day, as though it was some sort of parlour trick. Sadly, a lot of yoga classes these days are not really immersed in the true yogic sciences. I used to do it mindlessly watching television or listening to the radio at the same time and was not observing the correct breathing or attitude of mind of which Sadhguru speaks. In the few months of doing the practices as presented by Sadhguru, my life has changed.

I had retired from nursing after 46 years and I became morose and listless, asking myself, 'What was the point of me?' I was smoking and drinking every evening and feeling as if I might as well not be here. However, I was not suicidal and I still experienced moments of joy with my family, I just felt that I had lost my way. All that changed when I became steeped in Sadhguru's talks online and read his book *Inner Engineering – a Yogi's Guide to Joy*. I then embarked on some programmes offered by The Isha Foundation.

Chapter 10: Work and Friends

'Work is love made visible

And if you cannot work with love but only with distaste

It is better that you should leave your work and sit at the gate of the temple

And take alms of those who work with joy.

For if you bake bread with indifference

You bake a bitter bread that feeds but half man's hunger

And if you grudge the crushing of the grapes

Your grudge distils a poison in the wine.

And if you sing though as angels and love not the singing

You muffle men's ears to the voices of the day and the voices of the night.'

(From *The Prophet* by Kahlil Gibran)

I have been working since I was 13 years old and stopped doing a formal job last year when I was 70. I started with a paper round and delivered 53 papers every day, getting up before 6 a.m. and earning 12/6d a week (63p in today's decimal currency). The papers were very heavy especially on a Sunday and we were not allowed to ride our bikes on the pavement in those days, otherwise a copper would tell you off. Now you're regularly mown down by kids and adults on bikes and scooters coming at you along the pavement. I then worked in the shop some afternoons after school and on a Saturday; I can't remember what I was paid. I also had a go at waitressing which I would do all day on a Saturday and was paid 15/- for a whole day, and I had to pay National Insurance. I then went on to run the paper round session, having to get to the shop early to receive the papers from the wholesalers, organise the paper boys and mark up the paper rounds. I got this job when the previous incumbent collapsed and died in the shop – he was a nice old boy and his name was Mr Musk.

I left school when I was nearly 18 and got a job as a clerical assistant in The Inland Revenue tax office. I worked in the department dealing with Tax Reserve Certificates; I still kept up the paper round, going from the shop straight to the office. After three years of office work, which was very interesting, I felt I had to do something more meaningful, so I applied to do teacher training but I didn't have Maths 'O' Level, so I wasn't successful. I then applied to do nurse training, it was 1972 and there was a crisis in nurse recruitment similar to these days. I had an 'A' Level in English by then having done it by correspondence course, after messing up in school as previously mentioned. Prior to this, I had worked in a factory burning eyeholes in catheters with a hot iron. I also drove a van for a dry-cleaning firm, worked in a pub and did more waitressing. At one point, I had three jobs to go to in one day.

I was accepted as a nursing student and, though I was keen to train as a psychiatric nurse, I was persuaded to do the State Registration training initially. In those days, the schools of nursing were part of each hospital and we did six weeks in introductory block and then were released onto the wards, pretty much as 'an extra pair of a hands'. These days, students are in university and are supernumerary. My father, who had been a patient in the same hospital I was training in before being transferred to Queens Square for his operation, was very dismissive.

"Huh," he commented, "you a nurse? Nurses are born not made."

Dad did give me some advice, he said if you are doing an intra-muscular injection, go for a double top (as in darts)!

Sometime into my training, one of my colleagues told me that a tutor had said of me, "Lindsay is a born nurse."

The tutor never said it to me, so I suppose my colleague was being truthful.

I loved nursing from the outset; it is such a pleasure to care for people when they are at their most vulnerable. I can remember doing my first blanket bath; I did it with my friend Katie under the supervision of one of our nursing tutors. Poor old chap – he didn't really want to be disturbed but he was a 'soft target' and, after we finished and gave him a cup of tea, he looked so lovely and comfortable; he had really benefitted from our diligent attentions. I still have the first assignment I wrote about a person I cared for, written in longhand.

After about a year, I lost my way emotionally and left the training saying my marriage was failing which was true. The following year (1973), I decided to go back to the training. My marriage had failed and I wanted a career. I passed my finals on the first attempt and became a State Registered Nurse; sadly, one of my best friends did not pass so it took the shine off it a bit. But I do remember skipping joyfully down the road when I got my results. I worked as a staff nurse, first on women's surgery, then on a medical ward.

I then applied to the Bethlem and Maudsley Hospitals to do a post registration RMN (Registered Mental Nurse). I was so proud of myself for being accepted as The Maudsley is a centre of excellence and they only accept 25% of their applicants, well they did in those days (1978). I later discovered that they were looking for anxious introverts, so that dented my ego somewhat!

Incidentally, I met Jo Brand (the comedienne) during my training, she was at Brunel University doing a combined degree and RMN and we lived in the same student accommodation at The Bethlem Royal Hospital. That is an amazing place with beautiful grounds and an amazing archive with exhibits of famous former patients like Richard Dadd and Louis Wain. Jo and I used to go drinking in a pub in West Wickham with some of the other students. She was a scream then and obviously bound for greater things. We never kept in touch but when she did a stand-up gig at our local theatre recently, I was invited backstage and she greeted me as though the intervening 36 years meant nothing.

It was an amazing training which threw up all sorts of dilemmas and revealed a lot of my prejudices, opinions and attitudes. The training was designed to help you recognise and manage your own inner state before you could help others. One of our tutors was a formidable German woman named Gunna Dietrich BsC RMN. SRN. RNT. I chose her as my supervisor because I was frightened of her and wanted to challenge myself. She wrote a paper which was published in The Journal of Advanced Nursing (Volume 3 Issue 6) entitled *Teaching Psychiatric Nursing in the Classroom*. It describes the practice in teaching psychiatric nursing to post registration student nurses at the Bethlem Royal and Maudsley Hospital

School of Nursing, showing the exclusive use of experiential teaching methods. It was first published in November 1978 around the time I started at the Maudsley so you can see what we were exposed to.

I passed my RMN exam and returned to Worthing where I went to work in the only mental health facility in the area, which was The Acre Day Hospital. The day hospital had a prestigious history, being about the first facility in the country that took in voluntary patients; it was opened in 1955 in a beautiful manor house. This was a time when all patients were committed, i.e. hospitalised, under the Lunacy and Mental Treatment Acts and the Mental Deficiency Acts which were not repealed until 1959.

In the local psychiatric hospital, which was 22 miles away, there were around 1300 patients in the mid-1950s. The hospital buildings and grounds were extensive and had been part of a working farm. A farmhouse in the grounds was eventually used as a day hospital and had once, in the 1850s, been the home of Anna Sewell (1820–1878) who wrote *Black Beauty*.

I have a copy of a press cutting extolling the merits of The Acre Day Hospital, it being the vanguard of community care. The report is by a certain Hannen Swaffer, a journalist at the time, what a name! The big Graylingwell Hospital (near Chichester) had become a feared place where some patients were resident for decades and became totally institutionalised. Some women were admitted as being mentally deficient solely because they had had a child out of wedlock! I did work there for 12 weeks in 1976, being seconded for psychiatric experience during my SRN training. I was absolutely horrified by what I witnessed; I worked on one of the villas which housed 60 women, all of whom had a diagnosis of schizophrenia. The ward was a dormitory with a locker and a bed for each patient, there were no personal items for any of the women.

We had a bowel book and a bath book, having to bathe a number of patients each day. It was a soulless and depressing environment. A colleague of mine who had also been seconded was so distressed that she had to go off sick.

The sister on the ward smoked fags whilst she administered the medication and balanced her cigarette on the top of the drug trolley. I am sure that there was fag ash in the largactil syrup. It was at this time I became an ardent advocate of the anti-psychiatry movement and a fan of Ronald Laing. I did have a good social life mind you and had an affair with a gorgeous Mauritian student.

Mental asylums were considered to be total institutions according to famed Canadian sociologist Erving Goffman. 'They were a closed social system in which life is organised by strict norms, rules and schedules and what happens within them is determined by a single authority, whose will is carried out by staff who enforce the rules. They are akin to Nazi concentration camps, military boot camps, convents and monasteries. Some would say that criminal prisons are also total institutions.'

Everything was provided on site at Graylingwell, like a village, accommodation and entertainment – there was cinema showings regularly, religious pursuits, a beautiful chapel on site, work areas e.g. gardening and CSSD packaging (i.e. sterile supplies that the patients were paid to pack), and of course Occupational Therapy. The social life was the social club with subsidised bar for staff, or the

Naunton Pavilion Cafe for the inmates. Nepotism was rife as a lot of the staff came from the same family and supported each other in their recruitment and promotion.

I started work in The Acre Day Hospital in 1980 and worked there for 20 years achieving an 'H' Grade role of Clinical Nurse Manager, which I had to fight for when they introduced the clinical grading system in 1988. It took me a year, and my colleague and I won our 'H' Grades on appeal in 1989. I received nearly £1,000 in back pay as a result and took my twin daughters (who were four at the time) to the Ashram in India as I have mentioned.

I then worked as a counsellor in different GP practices dealing with my own referrals and then ended my career doing many years of full-time night duty in the new mental health hospital that was built in Worthing. It is a lovely modern building with great facilities and lots of glass to let in the light (it actually won a building award).

I stopped working when I was 70; I had become very disillusioned with all of the changes and demands that were being made on nurses by the Department of Health. My point here is that work had saved me, the discipline and the responsibility to oneself and others, the belief that one is making a difference. This saved me from a life of chaos. We talk about work/life balance as though they are separate – it is all life!

How tragic it must be not to love your work – go to the temple and beg.

Chapter 11: Personal Growth and Self-Development

The pursuit of wellbeing has created a huge industry, or maybe the industry has created the need in us to look to 'experts' for our wellbeing.

I went through a lot of existential angst in my teens and 20s as did most of us, and in the 1960s there was a whole new energy for change and renewal; young people were seeking answers and rebelling against establishment norms.

I guess if you are brought up in a Theistic system, e.g. Catholicism or Islam, and you don't question it (or if you are not permitted to question it) then you don't have to search elsewhere for answers, you just have belief. Sadhguru has said that you believe because you are unwilling to admit 'I do not know' and that I do not know opens up vast possibilities. I have already said what I think belief is; I was always seeking answers, although sometimes I forgot the questions: How did we get here? Why am I here? Who am I? Why is there so much suffering in the world? Why are there wars? Why is it so difficult to love others and so easy to hate or be angry? Why doesn't everyone agree with me? Why am I miserable or confused? Etc., etc., etc.

I first thought astrology and horoscopes (or horrorscopes!) were one avenue for finding answers. I read Linda Goodman's *Star Signs* and another of her books *Sun Signs* and I still think they are pretty amazing. What was I, a Virgo, supposed to do? What relationships should I cultivate – other earth signs? What did the position of the planets signify in my life?

I also explored numerology and the Chinese systems, I am a Pig in Chinese horoscopes and my life number is six I still feel that numbers are highly significant in one's life.

I used to express my confusion by writing poetry; confusion seems a common muse for poetic expression – it was for me anyway. Once in my teens I went for a walk along the beach at night in the rain feeling like a tragic heroine, and suddenly a policeman approached me, on duty and riding his police bicycle; he was concerned for my welfare. I went home and write this poem:

A Walk on the Beach
I only wanted to be alone
The wind and the sea and me
But no, a uniform, a voice
Is this world free?
Name?
Address?
Suicide?
Not me but I was followed
Is this world free?

How wonderful that a copper on a bike was around in the rain and cared enough to enquire as to my state of mind. When would you see a policeman on a bicycle these days – or even see a policeman?

Later we had the phenomena of the Mods and Rockers and I wrote this poem:

Basically Insecure

They stand in groups, uniformed
In packs, herds clamouring to be One of 'The In Crowd'
Scooters are their transport
They scorn those who are not uniformed alike
Individuality is drowned
In a sea of identical thought, dress, action
Almost like another race segregated
A thousand beings, yet all one.

It was 1964 when the Mods and Rockers were fighting each other on Brighton beach. If you become totally identified with a particular way of thinking, then everyone who doesn't think that way becomes 'the other' or the enemy. The Rockers wore denim and leathers and rode motorcycles and, of course, I was a Rocker. I bought my first motorcycle for £10 and it was a 250cc Frances Barnett; you could drive a 250cc motor bike on a provisional licence in those days. My fiancé had a Triumph Trophy – we loved the Triumph bikes and still do. I was stopped by a policeman when I was riding mine – DWF (Driving While Female); he thought I had taken my brother's bike or some male because it was unusual to see a female biker in those days. Or maybe he stopped me because it looked as though I didn't know what I was doing! I later had a works replica Dot and then a Suzuki.

Me on my husband's 650 Triumph Trophy

My Aunty Connie, my mum's sister, rode a motorbike in the 1940s and Mum would ride pillion. Connie came off her bike on a road in Ashdown Forest and broke both her legs; she was plastered thigh to toe but still managed to conceive my lovely cousin Nicholas. She said, 'Where there's a will there's a way.'

I'm veering off personal growth, but I must just tell you this as I'm talking about motorbikes. In the 1950s, the authorities became concerned about bikers; young men couldn't really afford cars, so motorbikes were it. Of course, conservative Brits were fearful of the 'Hells Angels' motorbike gangs and Marlon Brando's film *The Wild One* came out in 1953. The film was banned by the British Board of Film Censors for 14 years, so we had to wait until 1968 to see it! In 1967 it got an X Certificate and was first seen at the 59 Club in Paddington. We saw it in a cinema, and all sat in the front row because the opening sequence is the approach of a gang of motorcyclists and it felt like we were on the road in their path. Don't you just love the sound of a bike engine?

Incidentally, if you really want a rush, go to the Isle of Man TT races, probably one of the most exciting events ever, as I have said – if you love bikes. The amazing thing is that, as I write, Sadhguru is riding his motorcycle at the head of a massive gang of motorcyclists. He is travelling along the route of the Cauvery River which he is trying to save; it is called Cauvery Calling and the purpose of the bike ride is to raise awareness and funds as the river is dying.

Anyway, back to personal development!

The Beatles visited Maharishi Mahesh Yogi and started to explore eastern mysticism – I think it was only George who became engaged with it; his records with the London Radha Krishna temple are so moving. I love Govinda and he played with Ravi Shankar. The 1960s were so incredible, you can't really describe it, even if you were there, the energy of change was like a Renaissance and everyone had their own unique experience of it.

I read self-help books and looked for wise teachers, and I also did workshops and seminars. I did co-counselling, which is a grass roots method of personal change based on reciprocal peer to peer counselling. It uses simple methods; time is shared equally and the essential requirement of the person taking their turn in the role of counsellor is to do their best to listen and give their full attention to the other person. You could just ask each other what you wanted, just good attention or verbal interventions, there were protocols to be observed to make it safe. Ways of working are regression, catharsis, celebration, creative thinking, action planning and goal setting.

Some co-counsellors would offer workshops on a particular issue – I attended one on Re-birthing. Working with a partner, you got inside a duvet cover and they held the opening gathered up quite tightly. You visualised being back in the womb and pushed your way out through the 'birth canal'. As you pushed, your partner gradually loosened their grip on the opening. I had no birth trauma, so I just lay there curled up in the foetal position quite happily and then just decided to get going. We then had a counselling session on our experience. My partner had a powerful catharsis, his mother had screamed for a week after he was born and didn't bond with him; he had to do a lot of work on himself and so counselling really helped.

Moody Picture of my husband at the Santa Pod raceway

John Heron, who developed 'Co-Counselling International' from the original Re-Evaluation Counselling, was the head of the Human Potential Research Project at the University of Surrey. My colleague, Indira and I were fortunate enough to do some courses with John at the University. John had written a book called *The 6 Category Intervention Analysis* and it was just what we needed to enhance our practice as mental health nurses.

Serving the personal growth of the patient is the role of the mental health nurse or practitioner and happens with a relationship between the two which is almost entirely verbal. The '6 Category' system deals with six basic kinds of intention that the practitioner can have in serving the client/patient. Each category is one major class of intention that subsumes a whole range of sub-intentions and specific behaviours that manifest them. This means that the practitioner can have absolute clarity about what they are saying to the client, and the intention behind the intervention, i.e. verbal behaviour.

The categories are divided into two sets of three:

Authoritative

1. Prescriptive – seeking to direct the behaviour of the client.
2. Informative – i.e. imparting knowledge, information, meaning.
3. Confronting – this seeks to raise the client's consciousness about some limiting attitude or behaviour of which they are relatively aware.

(John describes confrontation as telling the truth with love – not the definition of confrontation that most of us would give! He once confronted me in a training session I was doing with him and he said, 'Are you aware how much you deny your true elegance?' Wow!)

The other sets of three are:

Facilitative

1. Cathartic – this seeks to enable the client to discharge, to abreact painful emotion, primarily grief, fear and anger.
2. Catalytic – this seeks to elicit self-discovery, self-directed, learning and problem solving in the client.
3. Supportive – This seeks to confirm the worth and value of the client's person, qualities, attitudes or actions.

Of course, there are far more sub-categories and details on each intervention throughout the book.

Indira and I did the 'Training the Trainers' course with John Heron and then, for some years, we spent a whole day with each set of SRN students to teach them about the six categories. We used a lot of role play and you would be amazed at what came up for the students who were struggling mightily to know what to say to their patients and what they were permitted to say in answer to questions, such as, 'Am I dying?' I can tell you there was a lot of catharsis in those sessions and we were so privileged to have that time with the students.

I wonder what they are taught now?

John Heron was a very charismatic and attractive man who was an inspiration to me and very influential in shaping my approach to my patients in my demeanour, grammar and manner of speech. John is now in New Zealand; he is 91 years old and is co-director of the South Pacific Centre for Human Inquiry in Auckland. His current pursuits are way beyond my scope; it's almost as if he is trying to categorise spiritual experiences. He will always be a role model for me with his towering intellect and his great humanity. He is a beautiful man and I fancied him rotten!

These were exciting times and so important to my work at the Day Hospital. It was there I met Gwen who was the charge nurse when I was employed there; she is a powerhouse, a wonderful nurse and a champion of the oppressed. Gwen challenged all of the outdated practices that existed in the Day Hospital when she took up her post. She was and is fearless and so accomplished in her dealing with authority figures, such as consultant psychiatrists and managers.

It was she who established the Day Hospital as a nurse-led facility where therapy groups and individual counselling were offered; she created an environment where positive change could occur and moved away from the 'medical model' of mental illness.

As she was employed by the Chichester Health Authority, she returned there when the Worthing Priority Care Service took over the running of the Day Hospital. She returned to work at Graylingwell and sadly was injured by a patient on a very challenging ward that was understaffed. Gwen had repeatedly warned her managers that the ward was unsafe both in her capacity as COHSE representative (Confederation of Health Service Employees) and as the ward manager (NB. COHSE was merged with NUPE – National Union of Public Employees and other unions to form Unison in 1993). She went on to sue the Health Authority for the negligence which had led to her being attacked – I don't know anyone who would have the guts to do that!

She had documented all her submissions to them and had written records.

The Health Authority had not been so diligent and the case went to the High Court. On the advice of her QC, she accepted their offer of compensation, virtually on the court steps. He pointed out that, if they went into court, the outcome was never guaranteed and that, given the contentious issues involved, it was not clear how the judge would rule. Her QC said that he knew she had pursued the case on a point of principle but that principles would not support her financially. The union that was backing her (COHSE) would have gone all the way and had the consultant psychiatrist and other brave colleagues who were prepared to go to court and testify on her behalf – brave because they were still employed by the Health Authority. She would have preferred her 'day in court' and would have continued with the proceedings but it had taken 7 years an she nearly lost her house!

Gwen was also very influential in raising my political awareness and my feminist views. We went on demonstrations, e.g. to a bomb factory (not one marked on any map), to Greenham Common and we attended various workshops that raised awareness of women's issues and roles in society. She is retired now, still an iconoclast and still my friend.

I got her job as Charge Nurse (sister) when she returned to Chichester and put all my efforts into maintaining the ethos she had created, along with my dear colleague Indira who was the other Charge Nurse (sister). Our work at the Day Hospital continued and we ran encounter groups, self-awareness, anxiety management and individual counselling. We also ran anger groups where we encouraged people to act out their anger (or abreact as John Heron would say). There is a theory that depression is anger turned inward. We ran groups on trust, art therapy, relaxation and meditation before they marketed it as 'Mindfulness'.

We had the most wonderful O.T. helper with us and her name was Brenda; she was an awesome woman and I loved her. Brenda got people working in the garden or making things and she also did some personal grooming sessions which really boosted the patients' self-esteem. She could turn her hand to anything and was always the first to come up with ideas, solutions and real practical support. She is sadly no longer with us, but she lived into her 80s, still doing voluntary work and I often remember her with great fondness.

When you run therapy groups, you are also doing therapy on yourself. But you can go on forever delving into your own psychology. You then become a therapy junkie, but you will still be poking around in the same old shit!

The mind is like a rubbish bin – put your rubbish in there but don't get in there!

It is never ending – don't go there – don't get stuck in your head!

In my pursuit of self-knowledge, I also found Louise Hay; she wrote many books, one of which is called *You Can Heal your Life* which espoused the mind/body theory, i.e. the mental causes for physical illness and the metaphysical ways to overcome them. Louise was diagnosed with cancer and advised to have an operation, but she believed that cancer comes from a pattern of deep resentment that is held for a long time until it literally eats away at the body. She postponed her surgery and did a lot of work to release the resentments she harboured about the rape when she was five years old and worked on forgiveness. She also went to a nutritionist to detoxify her body and the result was that the cancer was no longer present. To this day, if I have a pain or another symptom, I look in her book *Heal your Body* to see what unconscious pattern I may be running and I do the affirmation to help resolve it. For example, for ageing problems, the probable causes are social beliefs, old thinking, fear of being oneself and rejection of the now. The new thought pattern is 'I Love and accept myself at every age and each moment in life is perfect'.

My personal growth and self-awareness were much influenced by feminist writers such as Germaine Greer. When her book *The Female Eunuch* was published in 1970, it had a huge influence in raising women's consciousness; we had been aware of Germaine and her involvement with the underground press. I think she appeared on the front page of 'Oz' undoing Viv Stanshall's flies and was a staff writer on the paper. She also wrote very movingly about her quest to know her father in *Daddy We Hardly Knew You* and her book *The Mad Woman's Underclothes* is a great collection of her articles – including the memorable *Lady Love Your Cunt*.

With my interest in mental health nursing, I was also very taken with Phyllis Chesler's book *Women and Madness: When is a Woman Mad and Who is it that Decides?* This was the first book to address critical questions about women and mental health and the gender bias that existed (exists!). Then there is *Good and Mad: The Revolutionary Power of Women's Anger* by Rebecca Traister, published in 2018; women are continuing to redefine themselves. There are other feminist writers who were influential for me such as Gloria Steinem (85 years old and still active), Simone de Beauvoir and Betty Friedan (check out YouTube CBC, *One of America's Great Feminists Betty Friedan* and just listen to this three-minute talk).

One of the most powerful personal growth seminars I went to was the EST training, or Erhard Seminars Training. This took place over two weekends in a hotel ballroom in 1984. Prior to the training, we had been asked to clarify for ourselves what we wished to achieve from the process and then we turned up at The Great Eastern Hotel in London and there was about 250 participants and one trainer. At registration, they take your watch away or these days it would be your mobile! As the proceedings began, we were taken through a set of parameters for the training, e.g. only leave the room in the breaks, don't speak to anyone unless invited to do so and think about how committed you are to the process. The training was quite controversial and it had got a lot of bad press, saying it was coercive and about sensory deprivation. I thought it was amazing, a lot of the processes were internal, e.g. you brought significant people into your awareness and followed the guidance as to your relationship with them and asked questions of them. I got Mum and Dad and I asked Mum why she treated Dad so badly. I got my response immediately, as I realised, I was doing the same thing in my own life, treating them as inferior or abusing them for loving me as I couldn't love myself.

One of the processes we were warned might be particularly affecting for mental health nurses and to be aware of this. The process involved us circulating around imagining that we were in fear of everyone and feeling under threat. There were people screaming and some people vomited. I suddenly started laughing as I recognised that we were all fearful of others and all conducting our lives under some existential threat – it was a liberating revelation. In one of the processes, we had to walk on stage and gaze briefly into the faces of a whole row of people who had previously done the training, one by one. I guest there was about 15 of them and, as I gazed into each face, all washed clean and free of make-up, I was moved to tears by their presence and their total acceptance and love for me just as I was; it was a silent walk of joy and overwhelming humanity and had a profound effect on me. Of course, other people had a completely different experience of the process because of where they were at in their own life journey. Since that day, I can never really look into another person's eyes and not see myself in there, meaning, for me we are all one.

After the training, I was high on life, nothing and nobody were tainted, and the world was beautiful and so were all the people in it. I was transformed and I resolved to change my life. I finished with my boyfriend (Tim), with whom I had been living for three years as I have mentioned and embarked on a relationship with a chap who was ten years my junior, his name was Ashley (see Chapter on Sex and Boys). I also approached all the people I thought I had let down or hurt in my life and spoke to them about my actions and apologised and asked for forgiveness. I resolved to be true to myself and stop lying and trying to be someone I was not. I wanted everything to be natural and real.

I was talking to a chap in a seminar on Gestalt and telling him about EST; he was so blown away, he said I was an electric woman! He sold his car and took the training and ended up working with the organisation. I even arranged for the trainer we had, a lovely American guy who had been taught by Werner (sadly I can't remember his name), to come to the Day Hospital and speak to all the staff and try and get them to participate in it. My sister and her husband also went on to do EST and one of the consultant psychiatrists was going to do it but didn't follow through.

In pursuance of being natural, I stopped taking the contraceptive pill which I had been taking for nearly 20 years –I wasn't broody but I just wanted nature to take its course. When I told Ashley, he said, "If you get pregnant, you won't see me for dust."

I was 37 and had resolved never to have children as I didn't want to inflict myself on any offspring! Well Ashley continued to have sex with me and six months later I became pregnant. As I have said I had twin girls and my eldest daughter has the middle name of Esther because, without EST, I doubt my life would have gone the way it has. I pretty much did not see Ashley for dust, although he did come with me to register the girls' birth. Their birth certificate looks good; I was still married to one guy (John) and had children by another.

The state of euphoria lasted about three months, but I had no way of sustaining it or rooting it into any philosophy but then, in 1985,1 came across my first Guru. My dearest beloved friend Aileen had gone to a Satsang in a beautiful manor house and the owners were devotees of the Guru particularly the owner's wife who had met both her and the Guru who preceded her and gave her initiation.

At last, I had a Yogic philosophy and practice to follow which gave meaning to my heightened sense of awareness. The astonishing thing was that the Guru's predecessor, Swami Muktananda, had been sponsored by Werner Erhard when he did his world tour and went to America; Werner had visited Swami Muktananda in India and invited him to visit the US as a guest. There is some very toxic material about their relationship and *Large Group Awareness Training* online but, for me, I know they were both dedicated to the upliftment of humanity, albeit in their different ways.

Prior to doing the EST training, I had sought other spiritual teachers and was particularly drawn to Ram Dass, who had written the seminal work *Be Here Now* in 1971 and I listened to many of his talks on tape and also heard him speak in London. Richard Alpert, as he was known, originally was a Harvard professor and academic who, along with his colleague, Timothy Leary, were psychologists. They were engaged in experimentation with and intensive research into the potentially therapeutic effects of hallucinogenic drugs such as psilocybin and LSD-25. They were both kicked out of Harvard and Leary 'tuned in, turned on and dropped out'! Alpert went to India and found a Guru; he was named Ram Dass by Maharaj-ji which means Servant of God. Ram Dass is 88 now and still serving.(now deceased) I think Ram Dass said that he gave LSD to his Guru, quite a big dose, and his Guru said, 'Mmm, that will take you to meet God but you won't stay there,' or words to that effect.

My focus on personal growth led me to eschew other teachers and follow my Guru which I have done for 33 years and I think she led me to Sadhguru.

In 1973, my searching brought up this poem:

I am trapped inside this mortal shell
Should I speak and should I tell?
Spiritual hope needs a physical deed
The life of the mind can thus be freed
To express emotion, to act out hope
A concept revealed, can this body cope?
I must free myself form this mortal tie
Then the thought will be me, the product, I.

Where does poetry come from?

Leonard Cohen said if he knew he would go there more often.

I make no apologies that this chapter is all over the place – I was!

Chapter 12: Desperately Seeking Someone (Celebrity Worship)

On with the motley!

There has always been adulation of those more famous in our culture – singers, film stars etc. not sure why?

Sheila Kohler who teaches at Princeton says, *"Part of our curiosity is a way of learning what makes the great, great, in our own search for knowledge, fame or fortune."*

"In our society, celebrities act like a drug," says James Houran, a psychologist who helped create the first questionnaire to measure celebrity worship.

Now with social media we have near constant access to celebrity news. In the past, people have looked at monarchs for social or even fashion cues; the white wedding dress caught on after Queen Victoria wore one in 1840.

"There have always been status hierarchies," says Daniel Kruger, an evolutionary psychologist at the University of Michigan. *"Other primate species also keep a close eye on the dominant individuals in their groups,"* Kruger goes on to say, *"one is just learning what high status individuals do so you might more effectively become one; and also knowing what is going on with high status individuals, you're better able to navigate the social scene."*

Sadly, in some cases, this can lead to overvalued ideas when a person believes they have a relationship with their idol. This can lead to stalking, harassment and even murder. I used to fantasise about some pop stars but I am too self-obsessed to go overboard. For me, what this celebrity worship boils down to is: '*You've got something I want.*'

It started with Yul Brynner – I must have seen *The King and I* which came out in 1956, so I would have been nine. My mum loved the movies and in later years we were often watching the old black and white movies; classics like *Citizen Kane*, *The Third Man*, *The 39 Steps* et al – I still love them. Anything with Ronald Coleman or Alan Cuthbertson in, for Mum and I loved Gregory Peck, especially in *To Kill a Mockingbird*, with a very young Robert Duvall as Bo Radley – he was 31! Mum loved that movie *I Remember Mama*.

Anyway, with this celebrity stuff, Mum sent away for a photo of Yul Brynner for me – I thought he was such a beautiful man. My brother wanted a photo of Fess Parker who played Davy Crockett in a television series – maybe an odd choice for my brother but he was obviously attached to the character and his coonskin hat (i.e. racoon). He also had a deep affection for his doll which was called Little Black Sambo – can you imagine that we even called it such? It offends all our sensibilities now and smacks of the racial prejudice of the times; it was the 1950s and then it was presumed OK to have little golliwogs with our marmalade, even that word sounds hideous now. Thank goodness we have moved on from those times, but Peter loved that doll.

I then obsessed about Jess Conrad, a pop star who also made movies. I thought he was gorgeous – I saw him in a film called *Rag Doll* and fantasised about him and had pictures of him by my bed. He made a sweet but laughable record called *This Pullover*. He is 83 now and still looks good, so he has obviously taken care of himself.

In the 1960s there were so many pop groups and they all seemed to visit Worthing, which could never happen now as there aren't so many acts and the venues are too small. There were also some great local bands like The Detours and the Deltas – my sister and I were crazy about their vocalist, Chris, and then there was Steamhammer who did very well. Bands would come to the local nightclub, as well as to the Pier Pavilion and the Assembly Hall. I saw Lulu and The Luvvers at the nightclub at the start of her career and I have her autograph; she was absolutely exquisite to look at, so tiny and perfect in all her features. Strangely enough, I met her years later in an Ashram.

Johnny Kidd and The Pirates also came to the same club (a lot of performers had a gimmick in those days). Johnny looked really great in his pirate outfit with long boots, wide sleeved shirt, leather waistcoat, an eye patch and sometimes a cutlass; he did achieve fame especially with his songs *Shaking All Over* and *Please Don't Touch*. His pirate look was great and way before Johnny Depp but sadly he died, at the age of 30, in 1966 in a head-on car crash, and his voice was lost to us.

We also often had a visit from Screaming Lord Sutch who had 14" long straight hair which was mentioned in a newspaper – this was long before long hair on men became fashionable. Dave (Lord Sutch) would climb out of a coffin on stage and do a zombie walk towards the audience and then he would scream at us; we were only standing about 6ft away from him and sometimes girls fainted as it was pretty creepy.

He went on to form the Monster Raving Loony Party and stood for election on many occasions; the party still exists though he died in 1999 when sadly, at age 58, he hung himself (Dave would be pleased to know that there is a similar party at present in power in the USA). You can watch him on YouTube performing *Jack the Ripper*, his best-known song. I think he missed his mum.

Another band that performed regularly at the club was Dave Dee, Dozy, Beaky, Mick and Titch who had some great slapstick routines with brilliant timing. They did very well and became famous with their single *The Legend of Xanadu*. Then there was Dave Berry and The Cruisers – one of my friends was obsessed with him but she didn't class herself as a fan – she considered herself to be superior to a mere 'fan'. Once we travelled to Hastings to see him – his song *The Crying Game* still sounds good and is very haunting. My friend Annita and I used to get backstage as we knew the staff, so I met a lot of the stars.

Once the Yardbirds came to the Pier Pavilion at the time Eric Clapton had replaced Top Topham as lead guitarist and I remember Keith Relf was the vocalist. In the break we went to the pub over the road – I think it was called the Duke of Wellington – the original has gone but the site still hosts a pub/restaurant. Eric was sitting at the bar feeding arrowroot biscuits to the landlord's dog (in those days there was a screw top jar of them on the bar).

Eric was saying that he wasn't happy with the music he was playing and felt he was prostituting his art. We also saw Chris Farlow and The Thunderbirds and I remember that he had a huge American car outside the stage door (I think it may have been a Ford Thunderbird). I saw him a few years ago in a Worthing pub and his voice was still really strong – I think he's still performing at 78.

There were also some really good local bands like Uncle John's Band, Dirty Shoes and Desperate Dan and the Dan Band. Gone Cheese, which featured my cousin Nicholas, were also popular and played in the Starlight Rooms in Brighton; his mum, my Aunty Connie, was a great supporter and used to ferry them around.

Nowadays, my nephew Adam is a lead guitarist – he is really brilliant on the guitar and his first band was Fantasmagoria and then Swamp Donkey. He currently runs some open mic nights and is now in two bands, Hawkmen and Subterfuge.

There was so much to see in the 1960s and 1970s; Jimi Hendrix came to the Pier Pavilion and I remember his beautiful brocade jacket and frilly shirt. The Animals also played with Eric Burdon and Chas Chandler – the latter had 'discovered' Jimi Hendrix.

In 1968 we had the first Isle of Wight festival and in the second, in 1969, the organisers, beyond all expectations, managed to get Bob Dylan to perform. He had had a motorcycle accident in 1966 and had not really performed for three years; he treated the journalists like idiots in his press conferences – hilarious! A lot of celebrities turned up in the VIP enclosure – John Lennon, Ringo Starr, George Harrison (who got there first and went to Bembridge where Dylan was rehearsing), Yoko Ono, Jane Fonda and even Syd Barrett (bless him).

We went to the 1970 festival which got really crazy as about 600,000 people arrived. The Isle of Wight only had a population of 100,000 at the time and it was said to be one of the largest human gatherings ever – Woodstock only had 40,000! Unfortunately, some of the fans started breaking down the fences and ultimately it was designated as a free festival and was a financial disaster. The line-up included Jimi Hendrix, Miles Davis, The Who, The Moody Blues and Leonard Cohen. It's all a blur but I do remember hearing *Fanfare for the Common Man* by ELP (Emerson, Lake and Palmer). We could hear it as we arrived at Ryde Pier Head, which I think was about three miles away from the venue! *Fanfare* was from a musical work by Aaron Copland that was written in 1942 and it sounded absolutely magnificent.

Of course, Parliament had to stamp on this, and they added a new section to the Isle of Wight County Council Act 1971 preventing overnight open-air gatherings of more than 5000 people on the island without a special license from the council.

My dear friend, John May, was working in the 'communication centre' at the 1970 festival. I say communication centre, but John said it was a Dormobile with one phone line! All the press came in there to dictate their stories to their editors over the phone. John is himself a phenomenal freelance author, counter-culture journalist and editor and has worked in print for almost 50 years (just Google 'The One and Only John May' to see a biography and also www.generalistarchive.co.uk). He is awesome; among so many of his projects, John along with Ian Grant (ex-manager of The Stranglers and Big Country, amongst so many of the incredible things Ian has done), Rod Cohen, Andy Cowan-Martin and others set up Worthing Workshop. It was part of the Arts Lab movement in the 1960s and there were about 80 around the country. Worthing Workshop staged events, gigs, mini music festivals and 'happenings' and also had floats in the August Bank Holiday Carnival and was quite a force for the counter culture in those days.

We still have annual reunions.

I have always loved Leonard Cohen (rest his soul) and I saw him in Brighton in the 1970s – I can't remember the exact year, but I remember how funny he was, despite people saying he performed music to slit your wrists to! He sang gems such as *Don't Go Home with your Hard on*. In the early noughties, I saw him three times in a year, Bournemouth, the Royal Albert Hall and a vineyard in Adelaide. Cohen had retired in 1994 pursuing his study of Zen Buddhism and was ordained in 1996 – he left five years later. He had been defrauded by his financial manager and lost a lot of his money, so he had to go on the road again. His concerts in the latter years, before his death, were like an act of obeisance as he was almost kneeling down a lot of the time like an act of worship in homage to his fellow musicians (who were astonishing), his audience and to all humanity. He radiated love, respect and gentleness, how wonderful that he came to that before his passing.

"Ring the bells whichever bells can ring

There is a crack in everything

That's how the light gets in."

How brilliant that we still have easy access to his incredible legacy, like *Hallelujah*, *Anthem*, *Susanne*, *Bird on a Wire*, *Everybody Knows* and *Democracy* among many others. In fact, we are so fortunate that voices are not completely lost to us when artists die as we have a lot of their archive on the internet.

I think one of the saddest things that happened in the music industry, selfishly, was when Cat Stevens embraced Islam and thought music was forbidden. I thought he was already enlightened, living in joy and truth (well as indicated by his music at least). Just think of *Morning has Broken*, *Wild World*, *Father and Son*, *Peace Train*, *Moonshadow* and *If You Want to Sing Out, Sing Out* – such amazing songs. I do hope he is living in joy because he gave it to me in his songs. Thankfully he has found his voice again.

One of the most riveting performances I ever saw was Nina Simone at the Queen Elizabeth Hall on the South Bank, London. Robin took me there and it was just her and a piano. She had the most incredible voice resonating throughout the hall – it was a thing of profound and moving clarity. Similarly, Joan Armatrading was a stunning performer; her songs are so unique and moving and her voice has such an arresting but intimate quality.

Back to the 1960s, sorry memory is a strange thing – you never know when another portal will open and I haven't planned this much.

The Hollies came to the Pier Pavilion; we loved their vocal harmonies and such songs as *He Ain't Heavy he's my brother* and *The Air that I Breathe*. Anyway, we were talking to them backstage and Graham Nash autographed the top of my left boob – his idea! I don't know if Crosby, Stills or Young ever did that with their fans.

There were various trips to see bands. I saw Gene Vincent in a small venue, can't remember if it was Hassocks or Haywards Heath – I think it was the latter. Bless him, he suffered with terrible pain in his left leg after being injured in a motorcycle accident in 1955, apparently, they wanted to amputate and he refused so he had a limp and his left leg was often extended out when he performed – he usually wore black leather. In 1960, he was in England and he was further injured in a car crash that killed Eddie Cochrane. Gene had an alcohol problem probably exacerbated by his pain and apparently, in 1968, he tried to shoot Gary Glitter in a hotel in Germany – no, don't go there! Poor Gene died in 1971 at age 36 from a ruptured stomach ulcer – I love his songs *The Rose of Love* and *Say Mama* and The Blue Caps were a great band, Gene had enlisted in the US Navy when he was 17 and Blue Caps was a term used in reference to enlisted sailors in the Navy.

Ian Dury paid tribute to him in a 1976 song *Sweet Gene Vincent*; Ian was another musical hero for me; we saw him at the Hammersmith Odeon with his band The Blockheads – one of the best bands I have ever seen. I also saw David Bowie in one of his last performances as Ziggy Stardust; it was musical theatre and visually stunning. We saw Bob Dylan at Blackbush and they reckon he was on a flight back to the States before most of us had got out of the car park! Sorry I am in the 1970s again.

Back to the 1960s and Annita and I used to hitchhike to the Assembly Hall in Tunbridge Wells as their shows were on a different night and we got backstage there. I saw Howling Wolf there, his voice was awesome and he was a great guitarist and harmonica player. I love *Spoonful*, *Backdoor Man* and of course *Smokestack Lightening*. It was quite a shock when we went to his dressing room to ask for his autograph, being so close to such a huge black man, not a common experience in those days for me – he weighed 300lb (21 stone) and was nearly 6' 6". In that dressing room, he looked like a huge beast, defeated and far away from the plains of his ancestors. I know that sounds a bit trite but his presence and his talent seemed too big for Tunbridge Wells.

THE NIGHT TOM JONES CAME AROUND TO MY HOUSE!!!

Too many exclamation marks, but hey, it was 1965 and the night his first hit *It's Not Unusual* reached number one. He was performing at Worthing Pier Pavilion with his band The Squires or was it The Senators? I seem to remember the former name. I have never seen a man who could move like Tom did; his hips were so fluid and he was so sinuous – he would have made a great flamenco dancer.

Anyway, after the show, there were many adoring fans backstage and we were talking with him and he said, "Where's the action?"

I immediately said, "Back at my place!"

Bearing in mind that I was only 17 and living at home with Mum and Dad and my brother and sister. Tom was with his manager Gordon Mills and we got in their Jaguar and drove to my house; I remember them laughing when they saw the sign for Littlehampton (I didn't realise then that that 'hampton' was a euphemism). We got back to my house and I went in the back door to the kitchen where my mother was boiling handkerchiefs in a saucepan! I asked Mum if she wanted to meet Tom Jones – Mum loved him anyway and so they were welcomed in. If he and Gordon had been anything other than nice guys, they probably would have left there and then but no they came in and chatted to Mum and she made Tom a hot lemon as he had a sore throat (I don't know how we had a lemon). She also made them some sandwiches and Tom sat on the coffee table in the living room. I remember he showed me he had holes in his shoes at the time – he was just on the cusp of fame.

Gordon spoke of their proposed triumphant return to Pontypridd – they were going to drive through the town in an open car with Tom wearing some fantastic outfit – local boy makes good. Tom was about 24 at the time and I didn't know that he was married.

At one point, my dad came to the top of the stairs in his vest and underpants and said, "What's going on?"

I went up and told him it was Tom Jones and he said, "I don't care who it is, get him out!"

Then *It's not Unusual* came on the radio and Mum turned up the volume.

Tom and Gordon seemed genuine sweet guys and sadly Gordon died in 1986 of stomach cancer – he was only 51. I did kiss Tom a couple of times and I know he had a reputation as a serial womaniser but when you had such fame, it must have been overwhelming and women threw themselves at him. I acknowledge my own behaviour at the time was in that vein, although nothing happened between us and I still maintain that Tom is a genuine kind soul – you can plainly see that if you watch him on television. I'd love to talk to him now and wonder if he recalls that night.

Chapter 13: Nursing, Mental Health, Drugs and the 'Care' Industry (Or I Am Dying to Help You)

After 46 years in the nursing profession (I still have my dual registrations as I re-validated last year). I cannot begin to describe all I have seen and experienced in one chapter so I will give a brief idea of what I will say in my next book which will be entitled *Who Cares?*

The things I have seen and done in my nursing career will shock and enthral you. But I would say that, wouldn't I? I will talk about my own drug use in the 1960s and my own ideas about mental health care and the pharmaceutical industry. The following is a taster:

Substance misuse and addiction rates are no different among healthcare professionals (HCPs) than they are in the general population, but they demonstrate significantly higher levels of opioid abuse. Studies in the USA show that 15% of HCPs will misuse substances during their lifetime and rates of prescription drug abuse and addiction are five times higher among physicians than in the general population with especially high rates of benzodiazepine and opioid abuse (Butler Centre for Research 2015).

On 19 April 2015, the Express on Sunday reported that dozens of stressed out NHS workers have been suspended, sacked or disciplined for alcohol and drug abuse in Scotland. UK wide, around 100 cases involving substance abuse end up in front of the regulatory body, the General Medical Council, every year – which is a huge issue not being discussed. In 2010, a study suggested as many as one in six doctors were addicted to either alcohol, drugs or both.

On 19th September 2016, The Daily Mirror reported: '*Drug death capital of the UK revealed as the number of people dying reaches an all-time high.*' New figures from the Office for National Statistics show that the rate of recorded drug deaths is more than double what it was 20 years ago. Blackpool had the highest of drug misuse deaths nationally over the preceding three years of 19 in 100,000, Weymouth and Portland in Dorset came in second place with 10.8 per 100,000 over the equivalent time period.

According to *USA Today*, across the States, more than 100,000 doctors, nurses, technicians and other HCPs struggle with abuse or addiction mostly involving narcotics such as Oxycodone or Fentanyl.

In the USA alone an estimate 54 million people over the age of 12 have used prescription drugs for non-medical reasons in their lifetime.

On 3rd August 2017, *Health Day News* published a survey which found that 55% of Americans regularly take a prescription medication and they are taking more than ever.

In 2015, it was reported that New Zealand and Iran have been named as the countries with the highest rates of treatment for drug addiction in the world; but this applies to incredibly different types of substances, namely cannabis and opiods respectively.

The top most addictive drugs are heroin, cocaine, street Methadone and barbiturates.

Headlines in the UK correct for 2017/18 warn that over 11 million people (or 1 in 4) are prescribed potentially addictive medication.

After the Arms Industry, pharmacology is the next in being the most lucrative, the third being the alcohol industry.

Can you see where this is going? If we want a war on drugs, we should start with the Health Services! In my next book, I will speak of the attrition I have seen amongst nurses; one of my dear friends overdosed when mainlining Nembutal – she was a wonderful nurse. If you consider what has been done to mental health (psychiatric patients) in the last 200 years, in terms of treatments, either pharmacological or physical, you will be astounded by the evidence. This is since the medical men took over in that period. It could be argued that more drug abuse goes on within healthcare systems than outside them.

Psychiatry is the only medical speciality with a long-term nemesis – it's called 'anti-psychiatry' and has been active for more than two centuries, just read R. D. Laing, David Cooper or Thomas Szasz. You can also read about *The York Retreat*, opened in 1796 by William Tuke and The Society of Friends (Quakers); this marked the beginning of a move away from chains and fetters and it led the world in the humane treatment of the mentally ill (it closed in 2019).

As I have said, the breadth of my experience in the field of healthcare and my personal opinions need another book!

It is said that as religions crumble and people start thinking for themselves without a true knowledge of the reality of their own life and how to manage it in the most fulfilling and ecstatic way, they will turn to drugs or alcohol – it is already happening.

Chapter 14: Sadhguru

It was suggested to me by my dear sister that I 'check out' Sadhguru on the internet, this was late 2018. Following my retirement after 46 years in nursing, 40 of them in psychiatry, I had become morose and was feeling that my life was pointless. I wasn't suicidal but I lacked motivation and energy and was drinking beer every night and smoking my roll-ups.

I started to read about Sadhguru and listened to his talks; there is a vast library of his material online – just put Isha Foundation or Sadhguru into your search engine. '*The only way to experience true wellbeing is to turn inward. This is what yoga means – not up, not out but in, in is the only way out.*' (Sadhguru) I had been practising yoga for decades but Sadhguru teaches about the true science of yoga.

Jaggi Vasudev, a young agnostic who turned yogi, a wild motorcyclist who turned mystic, a sceptic who turned spiritual guide describes Sadhguru (this quote is taken from *More Than a Life – Sadhguru* a biography by Arundhathi Subramaniam).

My life has changed so much since I commenced my journey, following his teachings; I read his book *Inner Engineering* and did the online course and then was privileged to receive initiation with him at the Excel Centre in London over the Easter weekend 2019 for the completion of the course. I attended a course offered by the Isha Foundation where I was taught the Yogasanas.

I went to Geneva, to the UN, to hear him in a conversation about inclusivity and have just returned from Veranasi where I went on a sacred walk called *Bonding with Light*. My energy is high and I have written this book. I have become alive. Please check out Sadhguru for yourself.

Christmas selfie, 2019

Epilogue/Courses

The purpose of this book is to acquaint readers with my attempts to find happiness, contentment and joy and to hopefully alert them to the pitfalls. As I have said, it is also a call to follow the science of yoga as described by Sadhguru – I do realise that some folk may find that somewhat daunting so I am offering three programmes to awaken any participant to the first steps on the road to changing and enhancing their life experience should they so wish.

PROGRAMME ONE (one day)

Forget Name, Shame and Blame and Get in the Game (the game that is your life)

This is a one-day session from 10 a.m. until 4 p.m.

We will explore the significance of your name and whether you want to make a name for yourself or whether you think you already have.

We will look at the crippling effects of shame and blame in order that they can be acknowledged and released as those emotional burdens will weigh you down.

We will use role play and use experiential techniques to lighten the mood and there will be some laughing yoga of which Sadhguru would not approve – he is justifiably concerned that the term should not trivialised.

Participants will be expected to attend for the whole day, but their involvement will be a matter of personal choice; some folks are more ready and receptive than others and we will have respect for where each individual is at.

PROGRAMME TWO (one day) From Hope to Here Now – Are You Living in Hope?

Where is that?

Helpless

Obstructed

Perturbed

Emotional

We will explore ways you may leave '*Hope*' and move to '*Here Now*'.

Happy?

Enthusiastic?

Real?

Engaged?

Natural?

Original?

Willing?

Is your life going according to plan?

PROGRAMME THREE (two days)

The Full-On Freedom Formula

This programme is more intensive and gives you the opportunity to delve into your prevailing lifestyle patterns and habits; to explore where you are limiting yourself and how you may begin to create the life you have dreamed of. We will initially establish some ground rules as we need to work in a safe space.

Rescue Remedy:

Responsibility, religion, reality

Energise

Socialise

Create some choices

Understand your mindset

Eating, nutrition

Relationships

Emotions

Meditation

Escape and explore

Decide – desire/drink/drugs or dauntlessness?

Yoga – you did it.

This is the end, or is it the beginning?

Since completing this book, I have looked for a publisher and the process had become somewhat protracted, then in March of this year Lockdown!

I have been with my three grandchildren for six months, whilst my daughters have continued working.

My heart goes out to all who have been going through this pandemic, to my colleagues in the NHS, where I would have been working had it happened earlier and to those who have lost loved ones.

Another poem!

Something in the Air.

I thought I knew myself

I thought I was stable, steady grounded

I thought I was enlightened

Aware of the purity of creation

I thought I could face anything with equanimity.

I have been locked down, locked in, locked up

I have been found wanting.

My grandchildren have been shouted at, sworn at pushed around, put down, let down

Upset and frightened.

They have also been loved, hugged, listened to schooled and protected, fed and watered.

They are resilient, rebellious, stroppy strong strange, defiant, fun – loving dancing singing needing clinging.

They are here to teach me.

I am so blessed to have had the guidance of Sadhguru, through these challenging times, especially the live streamed weekly Darshan.

Who knows what is ahead? We will abide and we will prevail.

You are loved.